150 NORTH AMERICAN MARTYRS YOU SHOULD KNOW

150 North American Martyrs You Should Know

BRIAN O'NEEL

SERVANT
BOOKS

PUBLISHED BY FRANCISCAN MEDIA
Cincinnati, Ohio

Unless otherwise noted, Scripture passages have been taken from the *Revised Standard Version*, Catholic edition. Copyright 1946, 1952, 1971 by the Division of Christian Education of the National Council of Churches of Christ in the USA. Used by permission. All rights reserved.

Cover design by Candle Light Studios

Cover images: Ann Glover, Thomas Slatterwhite Noble 1935-1907, Collection of the New York Historical Society, 1988; Leo Heinrichs, photo courtesy of Wikimedia Commons; Kateri Tekakwitha, photo courtesy of Wikimedia Commons; Nykyta Budka, photo courtesy of Wikimedia Commons; Vasyl Velychkovsky, photo courtesy of Bishop Velychkovsky Martyr's Shrine, www.bvmartyrshrine.com; Francis Ford, M.M., photo courtesy of Maryknoll, www.maryknoll.org/timeline_images/1951_BpFord.jpg; Emil Kapuan, photo courtesy of Wikimedia Commons.

Book design by Mark Sullivan

LIBRARY OF CONGRESS CATALOGING-IN-PUBLICATION DATA
O'Neel, Brian.
150 North American martyrs you should know / Brian O›Neel.
pages cm
Includes bibliographical references.
ISBN 978-1-61636-551-6 (alk. paper)
1. Christian martyrs—North America—Biography. 2. Catholics—North America—Biography. I. Title. II. Title: One hundred fifty North American martyrs you should know. III. Title: One hundred and fifty North American martyrs you should know.
BX4655.3.O5423 2013
272.092'27—dc23
2013037602

ISBN 978-1-61636-551-6
Copyright ©2014, Brian O'Neel. All rights reserved.

Published by Servant Books, an imprint of Franciscan Media
28 W. Liberty St.
Cincinnati, OH 45202
www.FranciscanMedia.org

Printed in the United States of America.
Printed on acid-free paper.
14 15 16 17 18   5 4 3 2 1

To those who experience martyrdom today:
You are not forgotten!

CONTENTS

ACKNOWLEDGMENTS

Thanks to Louise Paré for conceiving this book's theme, and to her and Claudia Volkman for their incredible guidance. Thanks to Rosalie Grady at Downingtown's library. I kept her busy, but she always came through.

To my family—especially my wife—for their patience and forbearance. Also especially to my toddler son and constant companion, Liam. He made my work much less efficient. However, I wouldn't change a nanosecond of our time together. It was magic, and I thank God for what a great gift he is.

Finally, thanks to all who read the previous books. You're the reason this book exists (well, that and God's grace, of course).

INTRODUCTION

I hope you get two things from this book.

One is that many of the factors that led to these martyrdoms are by and large still with us. For instance, the state penalizes people for explaining pan-Christian moral teachings. In March 2013 the Canadian Supreme Court ruled that William Whatcott's fliers opposing homosexual practices constituted "hate speech."[1] Police in both Canada and the United States have arrested peaceful pro-life protestors, including a grandmother who simply sprinkled holy water on a sidewalk outside an abortion clinic.[2] There are also numerous lawsuits against Christians who simply want to live according to their beliefs. In our increasingly secular society, Christians face serious opposition to their faith, which conceivably could escalate.

There has been no loss of life yet, but we must wonder: Are the foundations for that unfortunate possibility being laid? As Pope Francis said in April 2013, "The age of martyrs is not yet over."[3] Regardless, as several popes have made clear, we Christians cannot let such realities inspire fear in us. Indeed, fear is from the devil. Instead we must "be not afraid." As we learn in the chapter on Servant of God Emil Kapaun (chapter twenty-five), hope is the only option in a dark and troubled world.

The other point you can take from this book: Everything you know about the history of the Catholic Church in North America, throw it out. Just toss it in the can.

Hmmm. On second thought, scratch that.

Why the ambiguity?

It's born of the fact that when I was asked to write this book, my first thought was, "North American martyrs? That's St. Isaac Jogues and company. Beginning of story, end of story."

That isn't the case though. You see, the first of those we traditionally think of as "the North American martyrs" was St. René Goupil, who perished in 1642. The first martyr on North American soil, however, died in 1542, one hundred years before. And one of the first persons executed on this continent's soil for being a witch was a resident not of Salem, Massachusetts, but of Boston. Her name was Ann Glover. She was a Catholic, and she was decidedly *not* a witch.

The men commonly known as the North American martyrs weren't even the first to die in Canada. That distinction belongs to Fr. Nicolas Viel, a Recollect priest who underwent a watery martyrdom along with an Indian named Ahuntsic in 1625.

Furthermore, mortal persecution didn't end with colonial times. A few years ago we passed the centennial of the martyrdom of a priest in Colorado, and we will soon reach the hundredth anniversary of the shooting of an Alabama priest by a fundamentalist minister. Then there are the many who died in Christ's service overseas.

But what about the North American story not being what you think it is (unless, of course, you're a serious student of this continent's history and the Catholic Church's role in it)? Whether it's the "tolerance" for which Canada is so famous or the real reason behind the American Revolution and the aptly named Know-Nothing Party, the answer to that question will unfold as you read this book.

Some of this is wicked, gruesome stuff, but compelling, awe-inspiring, and inspirational, too. So settle into your favorite chair (or even into your favorite pew at the adoration chapel), pour a cup of coffee or tea (not in the adoration chapel, mind you), relax, and enjoy.

The Columbian Era

In 1519, and in the name of Christ and the Spanish crown, Spanish adventurer Hernán Cortés conquered the Aztecs and thus Mexico, renaming the territory "New Spain." After the apparitions of Our Lady of Guadalupe to St. Juan Diego in 1531, Spanish missionaries in Mexico received millions of indigenous into the Church in the span of just a few years.

It took another two decades for the Spaniards to attempt evangelization of the land north of the Rio Grande River we now call the United States. Alas, these efforts were more challenging. The first permanent mission didn't exist for another thirty years. In 1565 the Spaniards established Florida's always-troubled Mission San Augustín. Spanish efforts never progressed north of Virginia.

Despite some impressive conversions here and there, various orders abandoned Florida in succession because of often-violent native opposition, French Protestant harassment, or some combination thereof. The Spaniards erected a network of missions in New Mexico, but these closed after a late-seventeenth–century revolt. Arizona bore little fruit until the Servant of God Fr. Eusebio Kino, S.J. (d. 1711), began settling missions there, of which there were eventually dozens.

As for Canada, the first of many French attempts to colonize the area north of the St. Lawrence River took place in 1534. However, every effort to establish a permanent settlement failed until 1608, when settlers founded Québec. Even that settlement's survival was never a sure thing. Savage Indian attacks, disease, and poor harvests all contributed to New France's touch-and-go viability. However, the French persevered and built a thriving colony.

As with the French colonists, so it was with their missionaries. After initial troubles they converted the Algonquin Federation and the Huron tribe, not to mention Maine's Wabanaki nation. However, the Iroquois proved almost universally unreceptive to the Gospel. This caused problems because the Iroquois were the most numerous and hostile of all the Indian confederacies. (For the purpose of clarity, the five tribes comprising the Iroquois Confederacy were the Mohawk, Oneida, Onondaga, Cayuga, and Seneca nations.)

Such tribes made many of the martyrs we celebrate herein. Some say religion had nothing to do with these missionaries' deaths. Rather it was a case of a clash of cultures and, in the case of the Spanish, their abuse of native peoples, and simple misunderstandings.

Was that really the case? Read on and judge for yourself.

CHAPTER ONE

Fr. Juan de Padilla, O.F.M.

+ DON QUIXOTE COMES TO KANSAS +

Some people have a willingness to try something new, maybe even something bold, but they won't do so without a safety net, some measure of security upon which to fall. Such folks typically do not change the world. Rather it's the people walking the high wire without the net who make a difference. Doing so is no guarantee of success, of course. For every Columbus we have thousands who failed in their attempts at whatever. Sometimes, though, those failures set the stage for some very big things. Such is the case with the Franciscan missionary Fr. Juan de Padilla.

We know very little about de Padilla's early life. Apparently he was a soldier from the Spanish region of Andalusia who left the military for religious life. Sent to New Spain, he held successive positions of responsibility there.

When in 1540 General Francisco Vásquez de Coronado (1510–1554) announced his expedition to find the fabled Seven Cities of Gold, Padilla and three other friars signed on to serve as the company's chaplains. Each wanted to evangelize people they might meet along the way, especially those of El Dorado, should they ever find that city.

Accounts speak of Father's thoughtfulness, civility, and vigor. He didn't extend these qualities, however, to anyone in the expedition who caused mischief or acted immorally. Instead those men would experience his cold gaze and gentle yet certain remonstrations.

3

While Coronado rested his forces on the Rio Grande for the 1540–1541 winter, Fr. de Padilla became the guest of the Moqui Pueblos. While he was away, Coronado's men captured an Indian who told them his land had gold, silver, and gems for the taking. The Spaniards were seized by a lust for lucre. The Indian was seized by a desire to get back home. To get there, he would tell his captors whatever they wanted to hear.

The party resumed its travels on May 3, 1541. Imagine the scene: hot, flat terrain, few encounters with area Indians, big open skies that rarely had clouds. How boring it must have been.

Since there was so much ground to cover and the Spaniards really had no idea how to get where they were going, Coronado split the party into two groups. Fr. de Padilla went with the group Coronado sent north. Neither party found anything, and they returned to Spanish settlements in Mexico.

Coronado tried again the next year to find the legendary cities. This time his forces took a shortcut and made good time to the land of the Quivira Indians, near what is now St. Paul, Nebraska. When Coronado decided to quit his quest and return to New Spain in April 1542, Fr. de Padilla stayed behind to evangelize the Quivira.

Sometime after Coronado bid him farewell, Father's hosts put him to death. It is believed he had gained a number of converts among these natives, who had come to love him. Then, however, he wanted to evangelize their neighbors and bitter enemies, the Guas. The Quivira couldn't stand the idea of sharing him with this clan.

Around May 1, 1542, Father set out with some unarmed companions. When he saw the Quivira approaching later that day, he knew what was happening and bid his friends to leave. They did and looking back, could see the Indians massacre Padre as he knelt before them, near present-day Junction City, Kansas.

Thus, a hundred years before St. René Goupil laid down his life for Our Lord, Fr. Juan de Padilla, O.F.M., did so on the Great Plains of what is now the United States of America.[4]

Why Fr. Juan de Padilla Deserves Our Attention and Devotion

When Fr. de Padilla bid, "*Adiós*," to Coronado, he gave up his only support system. It was a risk the quixotic Father took to spread the Gospel. Father knew that his was a win-win situation. Either he would convert the Quivira with his preaching or his blood would soak the ground, in which case it would become "the seed of Christians," as the tried and true saying goes. Father scored a double win, as both options came to pass.

O heavenly Lord, glorify on earth your servant Fr. Juan de Padilla, that by the light of his example, the number of souls who come to you and desire salvation through you may ever increase. Through Christ Our Lord.

CHAPTER TWO

The Florida Martyrs

+ HELPING OTHERS FIND THE FOUNTAIN OF TRUTH +

If a catechetics professor wanted a case study on how to successfully catechize a population, he or she would do well to stay away from early efforts to evangelize Florida's natives. The first Dominicans and Jesuits in that dominion had so little to show for their very costly labors that the superiors of these orders eventually abandoned the area altogether.

Amazingly, this lack of success did not translate as it did elsewhere into a significant loss of life on the part of missionaries. There was some loss of life, however.

FR. LUIS CÁNCER AND COMPANIONS

For instance, the first of Florida's martyrs were Dominican missionaries. It happened that these evangelists were supposed to go to the east coast of Florida, but their caravel's captain sailed them to the peninsula's west coast. He had strict orders to *not* do this, since western Florida had been the site of much Spanish-Indian violence. Authorities wanted to avoid the west and see if Christianity could receive acceptance using only peaceful methods on the peninsula's eastern seaboard. Why the captain disobeyed orders is anyone's guess.

The party landed south of what is now Tampa and was met by some locals who seemed very friendly. A convert named Magdalena served as translator for the indigenous, and she told the missionaries of a great village alongside a northern harbor to which they could take them. The date was around June 23, 1549.

Magdalena, Fr. Diego de Tolosa, a sailor, and a certain Br. Fuentes joined the Indians on foot, while Fr. Luis Cáncer de Barbastro, New Spain's greatest evangelist, sailed with two other Dominican priests for today's Tampa Bay. When the latter party came ashore, the Indians were still friendly, but the Spaniards were puzzled by the fact that Magdalena had exchanged her modest clothing for a native micro moss skirt. She told Fr. Cáncer that the others had become the guests of a local chief, and she had assured the Indians that the friars came with goodwill, unlike past Europeans.

Fr. Cáncer and his party reboarded the caravel. That evening crewmen heard splashing in the water and a Spanish voice asking to be hauled aboard. It was a sailor named Juan Muños, who had accompanied Francisco de Soto's ill-fated, murderous expedition and had somehow not only been left behind but made an Indian slave. He told them that Magdalena had lied to them. The Indians had killed the two Dominicans and enslaved their accompanying sailor. The Indians planned to make the other Dominicans martyrs also. They must flee.

His confrères encouraged Padre Cáncer to weigh anchor and sail for their original destination, Florida's east coast. He refused, however, because Tampa Bay had now been "hallowed by the life blood" of their brethren.[5]

For two full days Fr. Cáncer wrote letters, completed his diary, and gave away his few belongings. The next morning, June 26, 1549, he and the two other Dominicans rowed to shore, where some Indians stood ready to meet them. His companions frantically begged their superior to turn around, but as they approached land, he jumped overboard and waded ashore. When his feet reached the water's edge, he turned and gave a smile to his friends.

An Indian embraced Father, then put his arm around his shoulder and walked with him up a small dune. There more Indians surrounded Father and clubbed him to death.

FR. PEDRO MARTÍNEZ AND COMPANIONS

Another early Florida missionary was Fr. Pedro Martínez, Florida's first Jesuit martyr.

Pedro was born on October 26, 1533, in Teruel, Spain. His uncle served as regent to the Holy Roman Emperor Charles V, so Pedro was afforded an excellent education at the University of Valencia, where he earned bachelor's and master's degrees with honors in philosophy.

When he wasn't hitting the books, this hulk of a man loved to swordfight, and he partook in many duels. He attended Mass only on Sundays and holy days of obligation, and while he had a lukewarm attitude toward priests in general, he despised the Society of Jesus (more commonly known as the Jesuits). To his dismay, some of his best friends, men with potential and promise, entered the order, which at the time was all of thirteen years old.

Pedro's friends invited him to come and see for himself how great life was at the novitiate. He only went because he thought he could easily show them the error of their ways, and together, they would shake the convent dust from their feet. Instead, he met Fr. Jerónimo Nadal, one of the first Jesuits and a close collaborator of the Society's founder, St. Ignatius of Loyola. Something came over Pedro, and rather than ridiculing the Society, he asked Fr. Nadal for immediate acceptance as a novice. Father told him to pray and think about it for eight days and then come back.

This incensed Pedro. He knew that he was good enough for the Society. How could Padre Nadal not see this as clearly? So on the day that he should have returned, he opted instead for a duel that he had previously scheduled. However, the other party never showed.

Pedro thought things over, then went back to his apartment, packed his effects, and walked to the Jesuits' house. However, Fr. Nadal told him that the order possessed so little money that they had neither bed nor food for him. One biography tells us that Pedro "said he came not to eat nor to sleep but to work."[6]

Fr. Jerónimo put him on four months' probation and gave him menial tasks. At the end of that time, the superiors decided he would make a good addition, and so Pedro entered their novitiate on October 2, 1553.

He did so well that the Jesuits ordained him after only five years, well ahead of schedule. Following an assignment as chaplain to a military outpost off Algiers, which Muslims utterly destroyed, his superiors sent him to manage a succession of declining colleges. Fr. Pedro made each one prosper. He so impressed the Jesuit hierarchy that one superior said he was "of great virtue, industry, and bodily vigor, and gifted with the art of governing."[7]

In his spare time Padre Martínez held catechism classes for little children in the streets. He would encourage local nobles to assist him in the task. Given the fact that he was big and strong enough to have once stopped a bullfight with his bare hands, most probably didn't refuse.

One day, with remarkable humility, he asked his superiors to send him back to school. He realized that, in receiving holy orders early, he had missed out on the full extent of Jesuit theological education. That meant he might say or teach something that wasn't quite accurate and might, therefore, lead someone into error and from there into perdition. This scared him because, as he wrote to the Jesuit hierarchy, "If I go to hell," he stated, "the Society will not get me out."[8] And so he resumed his studies.

After completing this extra coursework, the Society sent their able priest right back to fixing faltering colleges. After dealing with two more schools, he recognized his heart's true desire was to serve as a missionary, particularly in Florida. He wrote letter after letter to St. Francisco Borgia, the Jesuit superior, detailing his qualifications and his strong desire to evangelize New Spain. In 1566 his boss wrote Fr. Pedro that God had answered his prayers: He would become a chaplain in Florida, which in Spain's estimation stretched west to the Mississippi and north to the St. Lawrence River.

A fleet set sail for the Americas in June 1566. Fr. Martínez would swing by rope from ship to ship, conducting catechism classes for the interested, dispensing the sacraments, and making up little rhymes for the sailors and other travelers.

When the flotilla reached Puerto Rico on August 11, all but Father's ship continued on to Mexico. The problem that now confronted Fr. Martínez's ship was that none of its pilots knew the Florida coast. The captain only knew that he would find the Spanish settlement at 32°. They were traveling blindly. Making matters worse, a hurricane blew them out to sea.

Things took a desperate turn when the ship's supplies began to dwindle. The captain got the ship close to land again and asked for volunteers to go ashore and find the local Indians. None would go, however, unless Padre Martínez went with them.

On September 14, the Feast of the Exaltation of the Holy Cross, Fr. Martínez jumped into a rowboat with two Spaniards and six Belgians (Spain then ruled Belgium) and pushed off from the mother ship. The craft landed on what is today Cumberland Island, Georgia. As the men searched the isle, another hurricane arose, casting their ship back out to sea. They would never see it again.

The men did not realize this. Not encountering any Indians, they waited by the shore, not daring to leave in search of sustenance for fear they would miss their galley. Fr. Martínez told stories and jokes and did what he could to keep spirits high.

Finally they deduced no one was coming to rescue them. They were on their own. They ventured inland looking for natives and found a village, where Father's charm and good nature won them help. These Indians directed them to the next friendly village, whose residents did the same, and so on. All looked as if it would end well.

That is, until they came upon Alimacani, a Timuquanan Indian village at the foot of Mount Cornelia on Florida's St. George Island. This tribe was friendly with the French Protestants who constantly waged war against the Spaniards for control of Florida. Our travelers had no way of knowing this. The indigenous, however, knew all about them, for a French Protestant living with the tribe had made them believe the Jesuits would try to change everything about them. By the time the Spaniards arrived, native hatred of them had been stoked to a fury.

It was October 6, 1566, when the Spanish party saw some Timuquanan fishing. The Belgians dared to approach them, even though Padre believed it unwise. Once they beached their boat, one of the Indians ran away from the party while the rest, roughly thirty in number, entered the water and encircled the craft. Suspecting no good, one of the crew's Spaniards, named Flores, jumped out, pushed his way past the Indians, and climbed a hill to learn what he could. Meanwhile two of the Belgians started walking toward Alimacani.

Drawing his sword as he returned to the boat, Flores menaced the indigenous with his blade and urged his Jesuit companion to get in the boat and push off. Had he taken Flores's advice, we would likely not know much about Fr. Martínez today, as he likely would have survived. Father, however, would not leave the two Belgians. He told Flores to retrieve them.

Knowing the Europeans were on to them, some natives grabbed the priest around his neck, choking him. Other natives took the remaining Spaniard and two Belgians to the shore, where they pummeled them until dead. The natives would have taken Flores too, but his quick swordplay enabled him to regain the boat's sanctuary.

Fr. Martínez was not so fortunate. The Indians hauled the large man to shore, and as he raised his half-dead hands, they brained him. Flores later wrote, "Surely he went straight to Heaven, where, please God, I hope again to meet him."[9]

Indian arrows took the lives of two more Belgians as the party began to row away. Exhausted and wounded by the ordeal, Flores and the two remaining Belgians languished in their skiff, which simply drifted southward until some Spaniards rescued them.

Other Jesuits came to Florida to evangelize the native population, but all met with similarly unsuccessful albeit less violent results. By 1573 the Society had left Florida for good.

Why the Florida Martyrs Deserve Our Attention and Devotion

These men did not die because they were European. They died because their killers were prejudiced against Catholics who fully conformed themselves to Christ.

How do we mirror these martyrs? Would anyone know we are Christians by our actions? Do we say grace before meals at restaurants? Do we say, "God bless you," to those we meet? Are we afraid to say, "I'll pray for you," instead of "I'll think good thoughts for you"?

We may not have to literally die for Christ, but when we witness to him, we can die in little ways that are appropriate to our state in life.

O Lord Jesus Christ, through consuming love of your sacred person, and for the salvation of your Floridian native children, the Florida martyrs gladly sacrificed their lives. Deign to make known that their works and sacrifices were pleasing to you by granting the favor we ask, and may they be thus raised to the honors of the altar.

CHAPTER THREE

The Five Georgia Martyrs

+ THE SANCTITY OF MARRIAGE WAS THEIR "OLD SWEET SONG" +

After the Jesuits left Spanish Florida in 1573, that colony's Indians had no missionaries to bring them the Gospel, for neither the Jesuits nor the Dominicans were willing to give it another go. For this reason, around 1577 Florida's governor asked the Franciscans to send evangelists. This is how Fr. Pedro de Corpa found himself in today's Georgia.

Fr. de Corpa's superiors chose him because he had shown himself ingenious at bringing native populations to Christ. They hoped if anyone could prove successful in evangelizing the largely untouched Guale Indians, it would be he.

The first mission established was Nuestra Señora de Guadalupe (Our Lady of Guadalupe) near present-day Darien, Georgia. Ten miles to its north, Fr. Blàs Rodríguez de Montes founded Mission Santa Clara.

At first things went well, and there were as many as fifteen hundred conversions. Because of this success the Franciscans added three other missions in 1595, the first headed by Fr. Miguel de Auñón at St. Catherine's—with Br. Antonio de Bádajoz assisting him because of his fluency in the Guale language—the next by Fr. Francisco de Beráscola on St. Simon's Island, and the last by Fr. Francisco de Ávila at Tulufina. These men built the missions as places where converts could live and get both their spiritual and temporal needs met.

While the Franciscans expected mission residents to be Christians, they did not expect them to give up their culture—except where it involved sin. Some converts understood that they had to put on a new man in Christ. Others, however, liked the idea of having their sins forgiven and salvation but wanted the freedom to keep sinning.

Such was the case with the Guales' heir-apparent, Juanillo, who had taken a second wife after his baptism. Fr. Corpa played John the Baptist to Juanillo's Herod (see Mark 6:21–29). He told Juanillo that, because he was living in sin, he could not succeed his father as king. After all, if the nation's royalty acted like pagans, what would the people do?

Padre's strong stance against polygamy infuriated Juanillo. He needed no Salomé to request the friar's head. He stormed out of the village and returned several days later with evil intent.

It was just after midnight, September 13, 1597. The well-armed Juanillo crept to Father's hut, accompanied by several warriors wearing war paint on their faces and huge feathers in their hair. Breaking open his door with the expectation of finding him asleep, they instead found him on his knees, his back to them, praying. Did Father know what hit him next? We can't know.

After decapitating him, the Indians impaled his head on a pike outside the village. In daylight Juanillo spoke to the people, saying, "Although the friar is dead, he would not have been if he had not prevented us from living as before we were Christians."[10] He said the Spaniards would retaliate and not distinguish between those guilty of Father's death and the innocent. Therefore the natives should kill all the missionaries. He said this would let their people cast off the yoke of Catholicism and give them the freedom to live as they had before.

The people accepted this remarkable argument and made their way north to Santa Clara. There they found Fr. Rodríguez. Father understood perfectly why they had come. He asked for permission to say Mass before dying, and they agreed, keeping him alive two more days in the bargain. During this time he told the Indians that everyone must die, and it did not sadden him to do so. What did sadden him was their slavery to Satan, demonstrated by their taking that which only God had the right to take, his life. On September 16 the warriors butchered him.

At St. Catherine's the chief was a faithful Christian. He sent messengers to Br. Antonio and Fr. de Auñón that warriors were on the way. The runners, however, never delivered the message.

When Juanillo arrived, the chief begged him to spare these good men. Juanillo refused. When it became evident what would happen, Fr. Miguel de Auñón hastily said a Mass. According to noted apologist Paul Thigpen, "It was the feast of the Stigmata of St. Francis, and the Gospel reading of the day contained the words of the Lord Jesus: 'Whoever loses his life for my sake will find it' (Matthew 16:25)."[11] Four hours later, the Indians found the missionaries and killed them.

Next they went after Fr. de Beráscola, an ox of a man. He was not home when they came for him, as he had gone to San Augustín in Florida for provisions. On his return Juanillo's warriors gave him a seemingly warm welcome. However, as the first man clasped an arm around his shoulder, the others attacked him with fury. After beating him into submission, they locked him in a cage. Three days later they butchered him, too.

Only Fr. Francisco de Ávila still lived. After he was caught in the forest, one of the warriors wanted his clothing and so spared his life. Instead of murdering him, they enslaved the priest.

Nine months later, the Spanish governor sent the military to exact retribution. This forced Juanillo to the town of Yfusinique. Besieged and defeated there, Spanish-friendly Indians executed Juanillo and twenty-four of his collaborators. At the same time, Fr. de Ávila regained his freedom and, returning to St. Augustine, wrote this tragic story.

The tale doesn't end here. In the 1950s, as the state of Georgia prepared to open Fort King George Historic Park, officials asked archaeologist Sheila Caldwell to excavate for the remains of the Guale settlement. In a trash pile she found a skull. Could it be de Corpa's? At the time no one could say, so the remains went into a box, where they remained for decades.

Taking advantage of recent advances in technology, Arizona State University bioarchaeologist Christopher Stojanowski examined the skull. He determined that it definitely came from a European man in his thirties. This would fit Fr. de Corpa, who died at age thirty-five. Also, the skull showed signs consistent with clubbing, scalping, decapitation, and impalement. It is still impossible to say, however, whether the skull is de Corpa's.

Why the Georgia Martyrs Deserve Our Attention and Devotion

Since the Church is founded on the Gospel given by Jesus Christ to the apostles, and Jesus is Truth—not *a* truth but *the* Truth—doesn't it follow that the Church should change the culture, not the culture the Church? Juanillo wanted it the other way around. Essentially that's the nature of sin. Juanillo was the same as any of us.

Thankfully, the Church is always ready to reconcile us to the body of Christ through confession. Granted, it's humbling to seek forgiveness, but the reward for doing so is huge: eternal life.

Lord of all, we thank you for giving us confession. Through it, give us the graces and especially the humility we need to recognize when our own way is not yours.

CHAPTER FOUR

The Texas Martyrs

+ ARE WE THERE YET? +

⊂∞⊃

This next story doesn't involve martyrdom per se.[12] That noted, four Dominican friars died in Texas in the most horrific of circumstances while serving their fellow man for the sake of Christ. As such, we can call them quasi-martyrs, because it was their dedication to Christ and love for all that put them in harm's way.

After both Spanish King Charles I (1516–1556) and Pope Paul III (1534–1549) outlawed slavery in the New World, the slavers simply moved their business to the black market. The Dominicans learned of this and informed the Holy See, which then asked Fr. Juan de Ferrer, O.P., to prepare an in-depth report. Upon its completion Padre Ferrer packed the manuscript and boarded one of four galleons that constituted the semiannual *Flota Plata* ("Silver Fleet"). Loaded with silver and gold, this flotilla left Veracruz, Mexico, on April 9, 1554, for Havana. After this it would cross the Atlantic.

However, around April 29, a hurricane blew three of the barques—the *San Esteban*, *Espíritu Santo*, and *Santa María de Yciar*—off course toward the Texas coast, where they beached on a sandbar near Corpus Christi, Texas. For several days the three hundred survivors lived on water and food salvaged from the wrecks, but then the local Karankawa Indians began attacking the castaways.

Casualties were few, but the assault convinced the party to flee south for the nearest Spanish settlement. They believed themselves only a few days' march from their destination, whereas it was actually a month's travel. Along the route, the Karankawa ceaselessly picked off the travelers. Once, the Indians captured two Spaniards, hog-tied them, stripped them, and then set them free. The survivors deduced from this that the natives simply wanted their clothes. Because of this, the men and women removed every thread from their bodies.

The menfolk gave the women and children a head start, both for modesty's sake and because the Karankawa had previously attacked from the rear. This time, however, the Indians launched a frontal assault, decimating the women and their offspring. When the men came upon the scene, the carnage shocked them. The Dominican friars—Fr. Diego de la Cruz, Fr. Hernando Méndez, Br. Juan de Mena, Fr. Juan de Ferrer, and Br. Marcos de Mena—tenderly cared for the wounded and gave the dying spiritual comfort.

They had little time for such work, however. No one knew when the next attack would come. Day, night, in the open, under cover of trees and brush, the Karankawa constantly killed castaways. After the first attack, when three Karankawa fell thanks to shots from the *conquistadores'* crossbows, the tribe lost no other men. The Spaniards lost their weapons crossing the rain-swollen Rio Grande, leaving them totally defenseless. Therefore they prayed over the dead and left them unburied, because the troop had to keep moving.

The company also endured many nonhuman assailants. At the time, average Europeans clothed themselves from head to foot. As a result, they had very fair skin. Imagine how easily this fair skin must have burned without the protection of clothing. When it peeled, the layers underneath burned as well. The sand scorched their feet. Mosquitoes relentlessly pestered them. Biting ants feasted on them.

Furthermore, the Karankawa arrows had stone heads. These did great harm if pulled out, so they had to be pushed through the body. This only worked if the entry and exit wounds could be cauterized. The settlers couldn't start fires, so once an arrow struck someone, it stayed.

In one attack several arrows pierced Fr. Hernando Méndez. To get away from the natives, he fled the river for the interior. There he met another survivor, a layman named Francisco Vasquez, who had made the same decision. Shortly thereafter the two chanced upon a black woman, whose name is unknown. She could identify edible and medicinal herbs and roots. She could also draw water from the ground. This kept Fr. Méndez alive for a time. However, the Karankawa killed the woman, and without her aid, Father soon perished.

Francisco Vasquez eventually doubled back to the ships. There he hid until a salvage-and-rescue party arrived. Meanwhile the Indians shot seven arrows into Br. Marcos de Mena, including one through his right eye's tear duct. Believing he wouldn't live, his sibling Br. Juan de Mena and Fr. Ferrer buried all but his face in the cool sand under a shady bush. The two then made their way back to the other survivors and arrived just in time for another attack. This raid claimed Br. Juan, the already-wounded Fr. de la Cruz, and nearly everyone else on the beach. By around May 10, of the original three hundred castaways, most were dead.

During this assault something strange happened, something very strange. With Karankawa arrows almost certainly whizzing by him, Fr. de Ferrer walked unscathed into the trees that abutted the coastline. He was never seen again. What makes this event even more intriguing is Fr. de Ferrer's prediction before leaving Mexico:

> Pity the ones that go to Spain, because neither us nor the fleet will arrive there. We will all die, most of us, and the ones that

remain will experience great difficulties, even though at the end they will die; except for very few. And I will stay hidden in some secluded place and will live some years in good health; but the importance of my trip is to fulfill the will of God.[13]

A few days later a quasi-miracle occurred. Br. Marcos de Mena revived. At around midnight he threw off the covering sand and staggered to the beach, where he saw crabs and birds feeding on his companions. Believing his time really had come, he ripped arrows from his body, including the one by his eye, and slipped into unconsciousness.

He revived when he felt something biting him—hard. Insects had laid their eggs in his wounds. Crabs were now eating these and his decayed flesh. Chasing them away, he stumbled to his feet and started walking. After a month he arrived in Tampico, Mexico.

Why These Texas Martyrs Deserve Our Attention and Devotion
Before leaving Veracruz, each of these Dominican friars had a reputation for holiness. By all accounts, they maintained that heroic sanctity by loving their fellow travelers as Christ would have: totally.

Life will inevitably present us with many opportunities to show completely self-donating love. Let us pray we never fail to take them.

Lord God, who are all good and worthy of all our love, please help us show the greatest degree of charity possible for your sake.

CHAPTER FIVE

The Eight Virginia Martyrs

+ VICTIMS OF A BROTHER OF ANOTHER COLOR MOTHER +

⌒∞⌒

When people think of the colonial history of the United States, most think solely of the British colonies. Yet the Spanish presence dates back much further. For instance, in 1526, eighty-one years before the English founded Jamestown, Spaniards discovered Chesapeake Bay, naming it Santa Maria Bay. That discovery coincided with an attempt at colonizing the surrounding region, which they named Ajacán. It failed miserably. However, the Spanish were nothing if not tenacious, and they made several other tries, including the last one, in 1570.

This brings us to our story.

Its main character is Fr. Juan Bautista de Segura, S.J., who was born in Toledo, Spain, around 1529. He received ordination at roughly twenty-eight years of age and taught at several colleges. He entered the Jesuits after eight years and was transferred to Valladolid, Spain. There he encountered such miserable, petty political intrigue that the mission fields of New Spain began to look very appealing. For some reason he believed that he could be holier there.

His superiors agreed to the proposition and, in 1567 or 1568, sent him to Florida as vice-provincial. When he arrived Fr. Juan Rogel and the district superior, a Fr. Martínez, briefed him on the mission fields. Fr. Segura asked about Ajacán, which likely provoked a patronizing eye roll. With things barely working in Florida, why waste effort up north?

That's just it, Fr. Segura countered. The lack of success in Florida after so much time suggested they look for other, possibly more fertile fields in which to sow the mustard seed of the faith. Didn't the souls living up north need salvation too?

And why hadn't the missionaries had more success? Was it due to them? By and large, no. They were fine missionaries. The problem lay with the Spanish soldiers. Young, virile men in remote outposts with little to do but get drunk don't often set the best Christian example.

Fr. Segura proposed for this mission a man he thought would be the perfect guide: Don Luis de Velasco. His sounds like an impressive Spanish name, doesn't it, maybe the name of a lord? Well, he *was* a nobleman—an Indian one.

In 1560, whether by force or consent, the young native had boarded a Spanish galley in Santa Maria Bay and been taken to Cuba, where he was catechized and baptized, receiving the name of his sponsor, Don Luis de Velasco. Then he was taken to King Philip II's court in Madrid. There the Jesuits gave him an excellent education. Now he was back in the New World, and Segura wanted him to return to his homeland and help the Spanish evangelists bring souls to Christ.

Br Juan de la Carrera praised Father's vision but objected to Don Luis's inclusion, saying one could not trust him. In his enthusiasm, Segura discounted this. Indeed, he predicted Luis would prove the most zealous of all those in the mission.

The missionaries landed in Virginia on September 10, and Don Luis made contact with his village. Meanwhile the missionaries built them-selves a rude shelter near the shore. Besides de Segura and Don Luis, the company included de Segura's chief aide, Fr. Luis Quirós; Brothers Gabriel Gómez, Sancho Cevallos, and Pedro Linares; novices Juan Bautista Méndez, Gabriel de Sólis, and Cristóbal Redondo; as well as twelve-year-old Alonso de Olmos. This youth had begged his father to allow him to accompany the missionaries and act as their altar server.

Initially things looked promising, with Don Luis apparently eager to fulfill his assignment and with the local chief even asking about the Gospel. The first problem, however, was that of food. There was little. The Jesuits had brought some, but they had to send half of it back with the ill-provisioned ship that had brought them to Virginia. This forced the missionaries into a position of dependence on the already-lacking natives. The Indians' farming methods were hardly advanced, and the Indians often ate more than they stored.

Whence the next trouble came would not have surprised Br. Carrera. As soon as the ship departed, Don Luis began distancing himself from the Jesuits. In fact, he eventually left them, supposedly to find his uncle at a distant village. He never returned. Too late did it dawn on Fr. de Segura that Br. Carrera had been correct.

The Jesuits believed death was not only certain but imminent. They prayed for strength, for grace, and for Don Luis's conversion. The Jesuits twice sent word to Don Luis, asking him to meet with them. Twice he refused.

And yet the Indians did not show themselves at Mission Santa Maria. Maybe they hoped that the harsh winter conditions and lack of food would keep them from having to use their hatchets.

In February, having endured over five months of increasing cold and deprivation, three of the mission party, including Fr. Quirós, went to the uncle's village. There they urged Luis to return with them, to turn away from sin, and to keep the promises he had made.

At some point the men recognized the fact that they were talking to the proverbial brick wall, and they decided to return to the mission. As they turned to leave, Don Luis gave his men a prearranged signal to loose a volley of arrows into the martyrs' backs.

Four days later Don Luis led several warriors to the Jesuit encampment, where they stole the Spaniards' axes. Armed with these, they attacked. Fr. Segura, who had always been so good to the assailant and who was his brother in baptism, lay ill in his hut, barely able to move. As Don Luis walked in, Father smiled and greeted him. The man responded by burying an ax in his skull.

The only person to escape death was Alonso, who fled to another village where a friendly warlord protected him. When the rescue party came for Alonso, they found the Indians who had murdered the Jesuits wearing patens and other liturgical items as jewelry and clothing.

Why the Virginia Martyrs Deserve Our Attention and Devotion
The Jesuits' expedition didn't prove the most prudential move in missionary history. Nonetheless, these men at least tried to make Jesus present in North America. They blazed a path. Furthermore, they were motivated by a sincere, even burning zeal to convert souls for love of Jesus Christ.

The New Evangelization calls us all to make that same zeal and love our own in the service of the Gospel. What are some ways we can do this that are appropriate to our state in life?

Lord Jesus Christ, place a burning love for you in our hearts. Let that express itself in a Holy Spirit-enflamed passion that yields service to people's spiritual and bodily needs.

Colonial Times

For our purposes, colonial times stretch from the 1640s through the American Revolution's end in 1783. Indeed, the majority of martyrdoms on North American soil occurred during this period, mostly in Spanish-held territories.

In Canada, persecution was primarily executed by the native tribes. Indeed, governmental persecution of the Church was nonexistent for most of this time. Persecution in the American colonies, however, was legion. By the time of the Revolution, Catholicism was essentially illegal in every state but Pennsylvania. Even there anti-Catholic sentiment effectively banned the faith outside Philadelphia. One still-extant Lancaster County church from this period was built to resemble a Quaker meeting house so it would not arouse Protestant ire. Canadian priests had to sneak into Maine to say Mass for the Catholic Indians there.

What about supposedly Catholic Maryland? Yes, it was created as a safe haven for recusants, that is, Catholics who kept their faith despite England's persecution of them. And so, starting in 1632, Catholicism had a toehold in the British New World. Nonetheless, a majority of residents were Protestants, many of whom were Puritans whose hatred of all things "popish" was legendary. Indeed, it was Puritans who outlawed Christmas and traditions such as the Yule Log in England for a time.

Perhaps it is not surprising, then, when, in 1644, Virginia Puritans invaded and conquered Maryland, expelling all priests from the colony in the process. Then, in 1646, colony Governor Leonard Calvert—brother of the colony's proprietor, Lord Cecil Calvert, Baron of Baltimore—led an armed force against the usurpers and reestablished control over the colony.

To prevent history from repeating itself, Governor Calvert introduced the famous Maryland Toleration Act in 1649. This gave freedom of religion and civil rights to anyone who professed belief in one God. At the time it was the most liberal law concerning religion in the Western world. However, in 1654, the Virginians invaded once again and revoked the Act and all other laws seen as tolerating Catholics. By 1656, though, Calvert had retaken Maryland. The legislature then petitioned the Crown to reinstate all legislation abrogated in the interim. The Crown agreed and made perpetual all laws previously enacted, including the Act of Toleration.

When William of Orange became king in 1698's so-called Glorious Revolution (more on that later), he effectively killed religious liberty in the colonies, even in Maryland. Between 1704 and the Revolution, the colony's legislature outlawed priests' sacramental ministry and said Catholics couldn't educate their children in the faith, inherit property, or purchase land. It passed laws requiring Catholics to essentially deny papal authority. Any Catholic who wanted to hold office could do so but could not practice their faith. "Papists" couldn't even vote. In 1756 the legislature doubled taxes on Catholics.

In 1760 Charles Carroll of Annapolis wrote his son and future Declaration of Independence signer Charles at school, saying that if he was younger, he would leave Maryland, so intolerable was the place for a Catholic. Only the lack of prejudice on certain judges' parts made life bearable.

In fact, here is how bad anti-Catholic sentiment was. Textbooks teach that "no taxation without representation" prompted the American Revolution. However, some historians believe that the two sides would eventually have resolved such issues. The real culprit, they contend, was the Québec Act.

"Say what?" you ask. "The Québec Act?"

Let's back up. Recall the French and Indian War (1754–1763). Britain beat France and thus obtained Canada. With the exception of some eastern parts of that dominion, Canada was entirely Catholic. Parliament found it wise to let religious dogs lie. Other than making government officials take the Oath of Supremacy, the United Kingdom did nothing to hamper the faith's practice among its new subjects.

Later, with rebellion brewing in America, London wanted to give its ninety thousand Catholic Canadians no incentive to join the likely seditionists to the south. Accordingly, it passed the Québec Act in 1774, which gave complete religious freedom to Canada's Catholics.

This was too much for the Americans, who called it a betrayal of all things Protestant. For instance, the "Suffolk County [Massachusetts] Resolves," which the Continental Congress endorsed on September 17, 1774, pontificated:

That the late act of parliament for establishing the Roman Catholic Religion and the French laws in that extensive country, now called Canada, is dangerous in an extreme degree to the Protestant religion and to the civil rights and liberties of all Americans; and, therefore, as men and Protestant Christians, we are indispensably obliged to take all proper measures for our security.[14]

Just before the Battle of Bunker Hill, the patriots distributed pamphlets to British soldiers arguing that Americans were justified in their rebellion, given the alarm they felt "at the establishment of Popery [that is, Catholicism] and Arbitrary Power [the papacy] in One-Half of their Country" [Canada]. Of course, the pamphlet starts off in a sober and measured enough manner:

> You are about to embark for America to compel your Fellow Subjects there to submit to POPERY and SLAVERY [sic]. [15]

Colonists labeled the king a closet papist, and New England citizens enlisted their sons in the cause of "No King, No Popery!" Speaking for Congress, Alexander Hamilton railed about how the "Romish faith" had become the established religion in Canada (a huge misstatement, putting it mildly), and how George III had placed himself "at the head of it." That the English Parliament would allow "arbitrary power" showed it had "no regard to the freedom and happiness of mankind" and was unfriendly "to the Protestant cause…. Your lives, your property, your religion are all at stake."[16] Continental Congress President Richard Henry Lee said, "Of all the bad acts of Parliament, the Québec Act is the worst."[17]

At the same time Congress told Québecois Catholics that it hoped differences of faith wouldn't "prejudice you against a hearty amity with us. You know that the transcendent nature of freedom elevates those who unite in her cause above all such low-minded infirmities." They held out hope that they, Protestant and Catholic, could live "in utmost concord and peace" and together defeat "every tyrant" arrayed against them.

Catholic historian Msgr. Peter Guilday seems perfectly justified in saying of this hypocrisy, "*Perfidious Congress!*" especially when one considers that half of the Revolutionary Army was Irish, the over-whelming majority of whom were Catholic.

Either ignoring or blind to all of this, the Continental Congress sent Benjamin Franklin, Samuel Chase, Fr. John Carroll (later America's first bishop), and his cousin Charles Carroll, Jr., to promise the Québecois that the United States would leave their freedom of religion untouched. The Canadians were unimpressed. After all, hadn't the British given them more than assurances? And hadn't the faith been prohibited and persecuted in all thirteen colonies to some degree? What would happen if a Canadian priest visited, say, Boston or New York and openly said Mass? Indeed, after France joined the American effort, New York officials arrested a French chaplain for saying Mass for his soldiers. Canadians justifiably believed Americans meant to "deprive them of their religion as well as their Possessions."[18]

"It is difficult," Guilday writes, "to understand how the people of the American colonies could have imagined it possible to win over Canada to a union with them against Great Britain when at every turn they outraged her people on what was dearer to them than life."[19]

CHAPTER SIX

The North American Martyrs

+ THEY LENT A HAND (OR TWO) TO EVANGELIZATION +

When we speak of North American martyrs, we typically mean the men featured in this chapter, mainly because we know so much about them. And because we know so much about them, they best make the point of this book: Anyone can become a saint. Seek to become one, and God will reward your efforts.

THE ADVENT OF CHRISTIANITY IN CANADA

The Jesuits entered the mission field of New France (i.e., Canada) around 1608. Catholic evangelization here started off very slowly. However, it was most certainly aided by the colonists, almost every one of whom was a sincere believer. It wasn't that the colonists came from some subgroup of über-Christians. Rather, living in a totally foreign environment with none of the Old World temptations made it easier for each Christian to live out the call each of us has to holiness.

Whereas in other nations' colonies the indigenous received treatment unfit for animals, the French showed "real charity for the Indians," even though they were "very possibly repugnant to them."[20] Also, unlike in New Spain, Indian converts in New France didn't have to worship in separate chapels.

Possibly this equality arose from the colonists' seeing what really lay behind the label "savage." You too might seem savage if your neighbors were constantly trying to destroy, enslave, and even eat you. Your manners might not be the best if you were always hungry. To put this in context, when Fr. Paul Le Jeune, S.J., taught some natives the *Pater Noster*, one Indian sarcastically suggested changing the petition for daily "bread" to daily "moose meat." They were famished.

Thus, the missionaries offered food to everyone and cared for the elderly and sick. And while the Indians came for food, they ultimately stayed for the love and the mercy of the God they didn't know made visible, especially by religious such as the Ursuline nuns.

Indeed, women religious effected many more conversions than did their male counterparts. A trickle of Algonquins had requested baptism from the latter. Following the nuns' arrival, conversions came in a steady stream. Interestingly, no sisters underwent martyrdom. There could be many reasons for this, but their presentation of the angelic and even (if you will not misunderstand the expression) feminine face of Christ has to rank chief among them.

Maybe more impressive than the colonists and missionaries were the Indians themselves. Despite their subsistence diet, they fasted during Lent. Keep in mind that back then, the Lenten fast called for daily abstention from all meat-related products. Also, the season usually occurred in the dead of winter, when growing or foraging for vegetarian foods wasn't easy.

After his confession an Algonquin convert named Ignatius demanded of Fr. Le Jeune, "Mortify me in public, so that those who wish to be baptized may persuade themselves that one must exercise virtue when one is a child of God."[21]

During their far-ranging and often arduous hunting parties, the indigenous often evangelized other tribes and fellow hunters. Each year the White Fish nation converged on a missionary settlement in an armada of canoes seeking instruction and baptism. Fr. Jacques Buteux, S.J., who became their personal missionary and later suffered martyrdom with them, wrote that the Holy Spirit "has made them more learned, without books, than any Aristotle ever was with his ponderous volumes."[22] He related that one year, a group demanded baptism after one instruction—from evangelists among their tribe.

Soon nations such as Maine's Wabanaki requested their own missionaries. And while conversion didn't change the tribes' "savage" behaviors overnight, it often softened them. A captured enemy might still get roasted alive, but the victors wouldn't eat human barbeque, as in previous times.

The amazing conversions were restricted to the Algonquin federation of tribes. The Iroquoian nations—not only those of the five-tribe confederacy, such as the Mohawk and Oneida, but also the Hurons—acted as a group. Either all converted or none would.

These peoples lived in what now encompasses lower Ontario, Québec, and upper New York. Especially for those in the New York region, their main contact was with Dutch and English settlers. These demonstrated no desire to evangelize them. They saw Indians strictly as trading partners. The natives resented the French because the latter trucked with their age-old enemies, the Algonquins. So while the Hurons had heard tell of this Jesus and the nuns and missionaries who served him, it was simply news to them, the same as if you heard about the inauguration of some obscure country's leader. That would likely mean nothing to you. Similarly, Christianity meant nothing to them.

At the same time, all Iroquoians, the Hurons included, wanted to be the sole middlemen for the French fur trade. They were seventeenth-century *Mafiosi* who would make *les Français* an offer they couldn't refuse. They thought it prudent to first try diplomacy, however. In an effort to curry favor with the denizens of New France, the Hurons invited them to send ambassadors, which is how three missionaries— Frs. Jean de Brébeuf, Antoine Daniel, and Ambrose Davost—came to live among this nation in 1633.

BEING ALL THINGS TO ALL MEN

It didn't take long for Fr. de Brébeuf to realize that, absent a huge miracle, he'd have no success evangelizing these people. For instance, while the indigenous allowed the Jesuits to build a chapel in their village, no one went to it, not even out of curiosity. The Indians had their own religion and let the French have theirs. As one mark of how difficult this made the missionaries' work, in the priests' first three years, they could claim only the baptisms of about a hundred dying infants.

Therefore, after much thought and prayer, Fr. de Brébeuf developed a brilliant strategy. With great patience he set out to become a Huron, to lose in their eyes his identity as a Frenchman. There was evangelization, of course. There had to be. This wasn't his primary focus, though. Patience, patience—with this nation, everything required patience.

The priests also found they needed patience with themselves, for one of their greatest challenges was that the Huron language is tremendously difficult to learn. After a decade of study, Brébeuf had only scratched the surface, never mind the Hurons' demand that one speak poetically. They were masters at creating metaphors, which the Jesuits struggled to master.

Slowly, very slowly, they gained the ability to converse, however, and the priests grew in their hosts' esteem. At some point the Jesuits became an accepted part of tribal life.

Brébeuf's plan was working.

And a good thing, too, for a flu epidemic hit the village. The Hurons fingered their guests as the cause, and for wreaking such havoc, the priests had to die. Even the missionaries' best friends in the village found this just.

At the council that passed the sentence, Fr. Jean spoke for the Jesuits. Here his years of struggle in learning the language bore fruit, for he spoke as any Huron would. He presented so effective a case that no one gave a rebuttal. Yet still the council sentenced the priests to death.

In Huron culture the condemned had the right to host a Death Feast on the eve of execution, sort of a macabre going-away party. They also had the right to make a final speech. Instead of again presenting his case, Brébeuf explained the Creed. He also revealed the fact that his ability to do good came from God.

The next day came and went, as did the next, and the one thereafter. Father had spoken so effectively *as* a Huron that the village never executed the death sentence. The saint had thus shown not only tremendous patience but also wisdom, as well, for after this, fifty Hurons wanted baptism. Beforehand, they couldn't comprehend how one could be a true Huron and a Christian. Now they had such a one in their midst. Once they hurdled that previously insurmountable intellectual wall, there was nothing stopping them from openly embracing what they had already embraced in the unseen nooks of their hearts.

St. Jean de Brébeuf

Who was this Jean de Brébeuf? He was someone whose stature and strength matched his name (in French, *Brébeuf* means "ox"). Born in Normandy in 1593, he entered the Jesuits in 1617 and received ordination in 1622. He taught philosophy at the Jesuit college in Rouen until 1624. He then went to New France for five years. Jesuit superiors recalled Fr. de Brébeuf to Europe, which greatly distressed him. He felt certain that he had done something wrong. However, he returned to Canada in 1633, and he was made superior of the mission in Huronia in 1634. In 1638 the Jesuits removed him as superior and sent him to a native group they called "the Neutral Nation" (the Attawandaron tribe). He returned to Huronia in 1644.

No matter what the situation, he was always calm and collected, even when someone tried prodding him into getting upset. (In contrast, Fr. Jogues was much more easily riled.) Brébeuf had tempests within him, though, to be sure: otherworldly ones. He wrote in his spiritual journal about how demons afflicted him. They took all manner of shapes and presented him with every temptation.

Fr. François Roustang, S.J., says the saint believed that this oppression came from his utter sinfulness, but Roustang seems to blame the harassment on an acute case of scruples. Maybe Brébeuf's problem came from the most demonic spirit of all—a conviction that God could not have mercy on such a miserable sinner as he.

Regardless, Roustang avers that God gave the Jesuit mystical experiences in proportion to his discouragement so that he wouldn't completely despair of his salvation. These intense ecstasies led to a growing longing for heaven and detestation of the world. Gradually his self-contempt abated. His demons faded, replaced by a subtle yet growing sanctity.

Visions of Our Lady, paradise, and the glorified cross certainly helped. He also gained freedom in comprehending that there was not a single thing he could do to merit his salvation; instead, faith is a free gift one can do nothing to earn. But his works weren't a frantic effort to, in essence, purchase paradise. Rather, as he noted, they were necessary but done for the love and greater glory of God.

By 1630, Brébeuf could claim that he had no temptation to any sin whatsoever. But what to do about all those past sins, even though he'd already confessed them? This is when he learned the depths of Christ's mercy and redemption. In gratitude, Brébeuf redoubled his efforts on behalf of Christ and pledged to accept any trials and death that his Master would send him. By the time of his martyrdom, he truly loved the cross, and with St. Paul, he could sincerely say, "It is no longer I who live but Christ who lives in me" (Galatians 2:20).

Satan, however, was not done with St. Jean. The devil tempted the holy Jesuit to the depths of discouragement when many Huron converts later apostatized. Father blamed himself. At that moment, though, God reached down and personally put his mind at ease. The demons never bothered him again. Now he could enjoy the fruits of his labors, not only the numbers of Indians accepting Christ but the quality of the converts.

Just as the Huron showed tremendous tenacity as warriors, they similarly showed themselves to be awe-inspiring Christians. Part of the warriors' training entailed learning tremendous self-control under the most horrible circumstances. The elders taught them to absolutely dominate emotions and any reaction to pain. When they suffered, they chanted to distract their minds. Now they chanted prayers.

Our Lord and St. Paul tell us to pray ceaselessly (see Mark 13:33 and 1 Thessalonians 1:17, for example). Most find this impossible. Not the Huron. A priest asked one convert how often he'd prayed during a daylong journey. "Only once," the man replied, "but it was from morning to night."[23]

Fr. Brébeuf's creativity, death to self, and perseverance set the stage for the Jesuits' baptizing roughly a thousand converts per year.[24] What an example for us in this time of New Evangelization.

LAISSEZ LES BON TEMPS ROULER NO MORE

As previously mentioned, the Iroquois wanted a monopoly on the French fur trade. While not opposed to middlemen, the French didn't necessarily need them. They didn't agree to the Iroquois terms, and the Confederacy could not stand that. This brings us to our next characters in the story.

One of those who came fairly early to the New France mission fields was Fr. Isaac Jogues. Born to a wealthy family of Orléans, France, the fifth of nine children, he went from being a sickly boy to being a robust, sturdy adult.

Possessing a decent facility with languages, Fr. Jogues immediately set about learning that of the Huron. Missionaries of this period also had to absorb another type of knowledge. Many noted how all the philosophical and theological training in the world wouldn't have prepared them for the radically different way the natives thought and how they conceived the world. Missionaries had to learn a whole different way of thinking.

Jogues came to New France a year earlier than Brébeuf. If you had known him prior to his first capture by the Iroquois, you might not have thought him an obvious choice for canonization. Why?

He never did anything special. He had no great gifts. He came up with no revolutionary methods of evangelization. He consistently played second fiddle, never taking the lead in any capacity. Unlike Brébeuf, he was effectively lazy with regard to learning Indian culture, and, as stated before, he was much more easily riled.

If Fr. Jogues was going to be a saint, it seemed he would be the patron saint of mediocrity. He appeared to be average in every way.

Except that he wasn't.

After his first capture, he bore the tortures that might have killed lesser men in an extraordinarily brave way, and he did so for love of Christ and thus of his torturers. After his escape, this sensitive man made the Bible's passages on suffering come alive as few people have before or since. Furthermore, he possessed an extraordinary capacity for prayer. He loved conversing with God.

And the seeming mediocrity? It was affected. He purposely let others take the lead and the attention. He only cared about doing his duty, whatever that was at the moment, for his duty in that moment was God's will.

Indeed, everything for Jogues was duty. He would have preferred living a very sedentary life as a professor, reading a good book or conversing with friends at night, smoking a pipe—sort of a Jesuit Frodo Baggins from Tolkien's *The Hobbit*. But the will of God as expressed to him through his superiors demanded something different.

CAPTURED BY LOVE

When the French decided they would not give in to the Iroquois' demands for a monopoly, the Iroquois established a trade blockade on the St. Lawrence River. It was a failed attempt to run the blockade that led to the August 2, 1642, capture of Fr. Jogues and Dr. René Goupil, a Jesuit *donné* (volunteer missionary), as well as their Huron allies.

About Dr. Goupil: He had entered a Jesuit seminary as a young adult but eventually left because of poor health. He went on to obtain a degree in medicine and become a surgeon. He also gave himself as a *donné*, joining Jogues on his journey to provide the Hurons with much-needed medical care.

When the doctor realized the Iroquois had him cornered, he didn't panic, despair, or try to run. Instead, knowing that wounded Hurons would need his skills, he prayed that God's will be done. Keep in mind, it wasn't as if he was clueless about what the Iroquois did to their captives. They were famous for their brutality. Still, he saw a greater good in staying than in resisting capture.

Fr. Jogues could have escaped, but when he saw the Indians had captured Goupil, he could not in good conscience leave. And a layman named Guillaume Couture rejected an opportunity to escape because he did not want to leave Fr. Jogues. When Father, Couture, and several others turned themselves in to the captives' guard, the brave could scarcely believe his eyes.

The Iroquois made everyone strip naked. Then each prisoner had to run a gauntlet, in which a hundred people on each side—armed with clubs, spiked whips, and fists—pummeled them. The three Frenchmen got the worst of it.

The next day the Indians began a forced march of the captives, covering two hundred miles in twelve days. As they staggered along, Fr. Jogues and Dr. Goupil catechized people and baptized those who were willing. The Indians killed one man named Ondouterraon the moment Father finished baptizing him.

The party finally arrived at the main Mohawk village, where Fr. Jogues, Dr. Goupil, and Couture had to run another gauntlet, even though this went against Iroquois custom (and these particular Indians were near slaves to their customs). The natives then placed the prisoners on the stage found in every Iroquois village. Tribe members wrenched out their fingernails with their teeth, stabbed them, and disfigured their fingers. An Indian man forced a Christian woman to bite off Father's left thumb. The natives burned his left index finger and so severely mangled the rest of his digits that even after healing they were a gnarled mess.

The Indians hated beards, so the braves plucked their prisoners'. They also tore out the hair of each man except Fr. Jogues. He was bald, a practically unknown condition among the Indians. This made them exhibit even more hatred and hostility toward him.

The Iroquois routinely sharpened their fingernails to very sharp points. These they dug into the Frenchmen's most sensitive members. Through all of this, Jogues said, he displayed a "haughty" attitude.

At some point Father held poor Couture, who had received especially harsh treatment because, in the Iroquois assault, he had shot one of them dead. The Iroquois interpreted Fr. Jogues's gesture as somehow applauding their friend's death. They thus put the priest through still more torture.

As evening approached, Jogues and Goupil were tied to the ground, and the Iroquois encouraged children to flip embers onto the prisoners' bare chests. Roustang writes that St. René got the worst of it. He lost his right thumb, and the only things recognizable on his face were the whites of his eyes.

Jogues also received nasty treatment because of the reverence the French and the Hurons showed him as the superior of the party. For instance, there came a night when the barbarians hung Father by his upper arms from two stakes in the middle of a longhouse. He later revealed that the pain was so incredible, he almost died.

One morning the kidnappers informed their captives that all would die by fire that day. Rather than feeling distress, the thought of being released from pain and of going to their reward filled each Christian—convert and cradle alike—with great joy. In the end, though, only three converts gave their lives: Paul Ononhoraton, Chief Eustace Ahatsistari, and a gentleman named Étienne. Their deaths were even more gruesome than the tortures described above. However, Chief Eustace died admonishing his fellow Hurons to forgive and make peace with their fellow Iroquois.

During this period Goupil and Jogues could have escaped, since the Indians often did not guard them. They wouldn't abandon their companions in captivity, however, although they may have wished they had. Once, during a failed Iroquois attack against Fort Richelieu, the French shot and killed two of the aggressors. According to Mohawk logic, two Frenchmen should perish for the two warriors who had fallen in the unprovoked raid. In the end, the Iroquois did not kill them—at least not for this.

THE MARTYRDOM OF DR. GOUPIL

For the length of his captivity, Dr. Goupil—whom St. Isaac had initiated as a Jesuit novice shortly after their capture—baptized terminally ill children. Knowing nothing of disease or medicine, however, the Indians believed that the Sign of the Cross hexed their offspring and caused their deaths. One such instance brought about René's martyrdom.

An old man caught the doctor crossing his grandson's forehead. This gentleman believed the doctor had called an evil spirit upon the child and that harm would thus befall the boy. The man told his nephew to kill the doctor, and here is how it happened.

Roughly seven weeks after the Jesuits' capture, the Dutch came with an offer to ransom them. The Orangemen may as well have tried making a working combustion engine out of twigs and vines. The Iroquois would agree to terms and then renege. They would ask for certain conditions and, when the Dutch fulfilled those, say that they had not asked them to do this. The truth was that Indian opinion was greatly divided. Many wanted to let the captives go; more wanted to kill them.

After the Dutch left and during the ensuing parley in which the Indians tried to work out this disagreement, Jogues and Goupil went into a meadow in the surrounding woods. Father sensed that this was the right thing to do but could not give a reason why. The two of them sat praying as the afternoon waned and the night grew older. Around midnight, they heard the village erupt in noise. They had no idea what caused the commotion. Knowing that discretion was the better part of valor when it came to dealing with the Iroquois, the two decided to simply stay put until things calmed down.

The next day Father favored escaping. They had the means to do so, and no one knew where they were. Dr. Goupil, however, would not leave the wounded and sickly Hurons. Father agreed to return to the tribe with him. It was September 29, 1642.

On their return they prayed the rosary. As they approached the village, they were finishing the fourth joyful mystery, the presentation of the child Jesus at the Temple. At the gate two braves confronted them. The aforementioned nephew smashed a tomahawk into the doctor's head. Goupil collapsed, repeating Jesus's name with his last breaths.

Fr. Jogues immediately knelt down, bent his head toward Goupil's, and granted him final absolution. He continued kneeling in anticipation of his own death blow, but it never came.

Jogues could not immediately bury Goupil's corpse, and when he came back the next day, some dogs had eaten a part of the body. Father took the surgeon's remains down to a water hollow on the riverbank and weighed it down with stones. He would come back the next day and inter it.

Whe he returned, however, Dr. Goupil's body was gone. St. Isaac cried for days.

MORE MINISTRY FOR THE LORD

Following his companion's martyrdom, the Iroquois essentially left Father Jogues to fend for himself. He managed to salvage some books from the things stolen from him, so he spent a lot of time reading. He also carved a cross in a tree and spent untold hours praying before it.

As for clothing, at first the Iroquois gave him only a soiled loin-cloth. The man who had stolen St. Isaac's baggage and was wearing his clothes took pity on him and gave him an old hempen poncho-like garment. However, it barely covered his sensitive areas and provided no protection against the cold. Furthermore, the rough hemp material rubbed against his bloody, wounded flesh, making the garment painful to wear. Of course, once he took it off, he got the worst sunburn imaginable.

Eventually the Iroquois assigned Jogues to a longhouse run by a prominent woman. The two got along so well, she took him in the tribal fashion for her nephew. The men in the longhouse, however, resented his presence. On winter nights, whenever he tried to take a spare deerskin to cover himself, they would filch it from him. The "aunt" eventually gave him a deerskin, and a French resident of the nearby Dutch colony gave him some warm clothes, but by then much of the winter had passed. In addition Father received little to eat. But forget the food and poor clothing—worse was the lack of privacy in the longhouse. If a couple felt like being with one another, it didn't matter who was watching. The same was true with people going to the bathroom.

Jogues knew that any of the Indians could kill him on a whim. Death threats were a regular part of his day. Yet at some point he realized he would live. With this realization came a drive to learn the Mohawk language and then use this to educate and evangelize. He taught the natives some science and debunked their myths, such as that a turtle had created the world and that the sun had a mind.

After a while, the Indians allowed him to visit the neighboring villages and minister to the Christian Huron captives in those places. The death threats and hatred never abated, however, either for Father or the constant stream of new prisoners. Many of these were Hurons, who were executed.

Once the tribe captured several women and children. One of the women was sacrificed to the war god Areskoi, and her body was dismembered and distributed to different villages, where people ate her roasted flesh. Fr. Jogues succeeded in baptizing her before she died, praise God, the poor thing.

Father blamed the captives' miseries on his own sins. And while his freedom of movement allowed the possibility of escape, who would have ministered to these afflicted souls? God had kept him alive for a reason. Might it not be to serve his fellow captives, no matter how unfortunate the conditions? In all he baptized at least seventy people and heard countless confessions.

However, he did ultimately escape, and it happened this way.

A year after his capture, the Mohawks made Jogues a manservant on a fishing trip. His party entered a Dutch village for provisions, and the *burgemeester* offered to help Father escape. Father asked for the night to pray about it, to which the puzzled mayor replied, yes, by all means, pray. Fr. Jogues only accepted the offer after determining that his leaving wouldn't adversely affect the enslaved Huron Christians.

While his captors launched a furious search for the escapee, the Dutch secreted him to the island of Manhattan. There, near Wall Street, a Lutheran boy called him "martyr." Jogues was the first priest known to visit what is now New York City. The treatment the Protestants gave him could not have been friendlier.

On November 5, 1643, Fr. Jogues departed for Europe, landing in England on Christmas Eve. The next day a ship deposited him on French soil. Almost immediately the man became a celebrity. Everyone wanted to hear his story firsthand. During a pilgrimage to Rome, Pope Urban VIII (1623–1644) gave him an audience.

At the time, the rubrics for Mass dictated how a priest held his fingers after the Consecration (that is, the changing of the bread and wine into Jesus's true Body and Blood). Given the state of his hands, it was likely that Fr. Jogues might never again celebrate Mass. So at their meeting, Urban gave Father an indult (special permission) to say Mass with his mangled digits. "It is not fitting," said the pope, "that Christ's martyr should not drink Christ's Blood."[25]

HIS LITTLE BLACK BOX

In April 1644, Jogues returned to New France. For two years he stayed at Montreal, helping found that city. Then the colony's governor asked him to serve as ambassador to the Iroquois at Ossernenon, New York, who had made peace with the French. With his superior's approval, Fr. Jogues agreed. The embassy proved successful. He heard confessions and baptized some Mohawks.

There was only one problem, and it led to his death. He had brought with him a black box containing a rosary, a prayer book, vestments, and a Mass kit. Now, it was June and hot. Rather than carry the heavy chest back to New York, he left it with his aunt, planning to reclaim it on his return. After his departure, though, an epidemic broke out. The Iroquois believed that the box was cursed and thus to blame.

In September 1646, some Hurons asked St. Isaac to accompany them back to Ossernenon. His superiors too wanted him to go and "ratify and confirm the peace." Fr. Jogues wanted to go to the Hurons; the Mohawks, however, were another story. The thought of once again living with those treacherous, vile heathen scared him.

Others would have refused. After praying, though, Fr. Jogues accepted his superiors' orders as God's will. And so it was that he left for Ossernenon on September 24, 1646, accompanied by the *donné* Jean de Lalande. He did not believe he would come back. He was proved correct in this. Less than a month later, he was dead.

Before continuing, however, let us first say something about his traveling companion. Lalande had come to New France because he was what we would today call a "survivalist." The Jesuits believed his skills would prove useful for the embassy.

En route the party discovered that the Mohawk Bear clan was on the warpath. Their Indian escorts abandoned them, but the two Frenchmen and a Huron ambassador pressed forward.

Upon reaching Ossernenon on October 17, the Mohawks captured and stripped Fr. Jogues, de Lalande, and the envoy. The next day Jogues, who was staying in his aunt's longhouse, was invited to dinner in another. By now he knew they blamed him for the calamities that had struck their tribe since June. If he refused the invitation, he risked insulting the hosts, which could lead to his death. If he accepted, he knew they could ambush and kill him.

And when he accepted, that's exactly what they did. As Fr. Jogues bent to enter the longhouse of his putative host, a tomahawk split his skull. Besides the truism about the blood of martyrs, if we can say anything good about his passing it is that, unlike his first stay with the Iroquois, he experienced no torture but rather instantaneous death.

His killers dumped his body in the middle of the village. Although the aunt told de Lalande not to leave the longhouse, he felt compelled to attempt a look at Jogues's body. Lalande stuck his head outside the house, and down came some brave's ax, immediately killing him.

The Mohawks placed both saints' heads on pikes along the village walls and dumped their bodies into the river.

THE OTHER MARTYRS

Jogues's death unleashed a demonic, anti-Christian war lust in the Mohawks, who immediately attacked the French and Algonquin. They slew Piscaret, an Algonquin Christian chief, and crucified a French child near Montreal. They also steadily attacked every mission village in Huronia.

A musket ball fired by a Mohawk killed Fr. Antoine Daniel at Mission St. Joseph on December 7, 1649. Amazingly, he had gone out to meet the assailants with a cross lifted high. This created a diversion, allowing at least some Hurons to escape. Just prior to their being slain, Fr. Daniel baptized several hundred Hurons, who thus died Christians.

Next the Iroquois reduced St. Ignace to glowing embers. Then, on the Feast of the Immaculate Conception, Sainte-Marie fell. Fr. Noël Chabanel had staffed that mission. Born in 1613, he entered the Jesuits shortly after his seventeenth birthday. He arrived in Québec on August 15, 1643, the Feast of Our Lady's Assumption.

History does not tell us much about Fr. Chabanel. What it does tell us is that he utterly disdained the Hurons, finding them coarse, savage, ignorant, rude, and beastly. Their looks he found revolting; their language, contemptible (after five years Father had learned barely any of the Huron language); their food, barely edible. Possibly worst of all: They had no wine.

The priest didn't much like the mission at Sainte-Marie either. He pined for a bed. He got one: The ground. And the longhouses in which he stayed were not weather tight, so he often awoke covered in snow. Furthermore, they were always filled with smoke. As mentioned elsewhere, they afforded no privacy and afforded a never-ending circus of noises.

Roustang writes that if one's love for God is strong, it will bear any hardship. One can infer he didn't think Fr. Chabanel possessed a sufficiently strong love for our Lord. If that is true, then what kept the missionary going?

First, he must have loved God enough to want to evangelize these people. Second, it was very simple: Serving them was his duty, and like St. Isaac, St. Noël was a man dedicated to doing his duty. Nevertheless, he disliked the Hurons so much that several times he almost broke and begged his superiors to send him back to France.

To cut off that option, he took a personal oath of stability, which meant he would never leave Canada. He also prayed for martyrdom. When that came it was a humble, hidden death, out in the forest. There this sturdy tree of a Christian was felled by an apostate Huron's ax.

Following this, St. Louis fell, and this is where Frs. Brébeuf and Gabriel Lalémant met their ends. Their killers ate the former's heart and replaced the latter's eyes with burning coals. As for the particulars of their deaths, they consist of so many obscene and barbaric tortures, one cannot prudently list them. What is worse, many of their tormentors were apostates.

Of Lalémant, not much is known of him, either. He was Fr. René's nephew and a scholar. He had wanted to serve as a missionary in New France. However, poor health kept this from happening for quite some time. We also know his death took longer than Brébeuf's.

We know much more about St. Charles Garnier. He was something of a prodigy when it came to learning languages. He was from a very close family but for his relationship with his father. His mother had died quite young, and his dad became something of an overbearing "father hen," if you will. Making matters worse, Dad always compared Charles's weaknesses to his brothers' strengths. Still, Pop couldn't have done too badly: Three of his sons entered religious life.

Mr. Garnier did not want Charles to enter the priesthood, and he especially objected to his son's becoming a missionary at Québec. This only made Charles want even more to serve as a missionary.

Yet he loved his father dearly. Nonetheless, around 1638 the priest wrote his father, basically telling him, "Look, I'm fine. Stop asking about my health." He then made a possibly not-so-subtle dig, writing that some ought to look less toward their physical health and more toward the health of their souls so that they not end up in hell. Roustang proposes that this would have cut Monsieur Garnier to the quick.

Roustang also thinks Garnier's lack of a beard was significant. Beardlessness was seen as repugnant in European fashion, and Père Garnier always rode his son about it. However, the Indians found it comely, and it is possible that this condition helped them more readily accept him.

Everything Charles wrote to his dad seems to be tinged with resentment and hostility. One wonders, did he recognize this as a violation of the fourth commandment and confess it accordingly, or like so many of us, did he rationalize his actions? Granted, his father had intimated that, *sans* beard and of weak health, his son might not be quite the man. Almost no son would accept this meekly and without emotion. How many males can identify with the hurt and resentment such a paternal assessment seems to have fired in the kiln of St. Charles's heart? Still, the fourth commandment is just that, a commandment, not a suggestion.

Thus Charles entered Canada with the proverbial chip on his shoulder. It seems his aim was as much to prove his manliness as to serve and save souls for God. He wanted to prove he could handle anything. If something was easy, forget it. He wanted to show he was tough.

So during an epidemic, when no one else would go out for fear of contracting the disease, Garnier not only went, he did so to the very Indians who blamed the French for their illness and thus wanted to kill them all. His charitable efforts opened hearts that might have otherwise stayed closed.

But the priest's spiritual life did not match his courage and zeal. Unlike Brébeuf and Jogues, he was not hell-bent on heaven. He didn't want God for his best buddy. This isn't to say that he wasn't in love with God. Paradoxically he was, but in a different way than that of most of his confrères. Roustang judges him as so emotionally stunted as to be incapable of rising to a higher relationship with Christ.

Indeed, he was somewhat legalistic in his faith. Roustang tells us that if Fr. Garnier believed union with God required X, Y, and Z, he did that, but almost in the manner of checking off items on a list rather than striving for the end of this effort, namely the aforementioned relationship with the Almighty.

Part of Charles's problem was that he didn't believe God was capable of loving him. He had to work to make himself accept the fact that our Lord *did* have this capacity. He eventually succeeded, and he became a great missionary. His zeal and effort to prove himself mellowed into a tempered ardor that bore results. He never said anything unkind to an Indian, even if he felt like it. He would also stick up for the indigenous if others spoke ill of them.

And as one who felt so wounded by his father, he worked hard to ensure that he never made others feel similarly belittled. Many who have been dominated in turn feel a need to dominate. Not Fr. Garnier.

Furthermore, while the young Charles had a problem with his father's authority, this was not the case with Fr. Garnier's Jesuit superiors. To them he perfectly sacrificed his own will, seeing it as that of God. If called upon to perform the most menial task, he happily did it.

In early December 1649, the Iroquois savagely attacked the village of St. John, where Fr. Garnier had established a mission in 1641. Father went about caring for the wounded and dying, baptizing many of the latter, until he was struck by two bullets. Still alive, he tried to crawl to the aid of a wounded man nearby. Then a tomahawk blow to the skull killed him.

Fr. Chabanel and Fr. Garnier seem like the least perfect—maybe the most human?—of all the traditionally grouped North American martyrs. And yet they are saints. Many reading this will find themselves in one of their portraits. If you do, let these saints give you hope and courage. They show us sanctity is possible for everyone because of, yes, God's love, out of which flows his ever-enduring mercy. Character flaws aren't important; what count are one's efforts for Christ. Keep our Lord as your true north, and you will triumph in the same way these martyrs did.

Why the North American Martyrs Deserve Our Attention and Devotion
Like these great martyrs, North American Christians today find their faith under attack. Our times overflow with hubris and suffer from lack of modesty and wisdom. This has led to unconscionable treatment of the unborn, the elderly, and the marginalized. Will history not call our culture savage and barbaric? God help our descendants if it doesn't. These saints show us that conversion—first our own and then others'—is the only antidote for what ails our era.

These martyrs also help us recognize something else: In life, they were not perfect. We're not perfect, either, but like them, we're called to be saints. "Let us also lay aside every weight, and sin which clings so closely, and let us run with perseverance the race that is set before us, looking to Jesus the pioneer and perfecter of our faith, who for the joy that was set before him endured the cross, despising the shame, and is seated at the right hand of the throne of God" (Hebrews 12:1–2).

Father, you have willed that we live in an epoch where all bets are off. People judge the wisdom of the ages as nonsense simply because it was not created in our image. Consequently, we can sometimes feel unmoored, lost, disoriented. Please help us follow closely in these martyrs' footsteps, which are really your footsteps. That way we will never go astray from the path you have laid for us.

Furthermore, as you did with these martyrs, give us new insights into how to love people into your kingdom. As you did with these martyrs, help us lay down our lives for others for the sake of the Gospel. And as you did with these martyrs, help us persevere, planting seeds that might bear fruit in future generations.

CHAPTER SEVEN

St. Kateri Tekakwitha
+ HOLINESS IS A NATIVE THING +

Some will wonder why one of North America's newest saints who died a natural death is included in a book on martyrs.

But she was a martyr, a *white* martyr. That means that she didn't spill her blood for the faith but, because of spiritual blackmail, always had to choose between her faith and what others wanted her to do if she was to live in peace. And always she chose her faith.

"She" is St. Kateri Tekakwitha. Her Mohawk father, Kenneronkwa, had married Tagaskouita, an Algonquin Christian woman, possibly as a result of the two tribes joining for a hunting party one year. (Author Daniel Sargent is adamant that there were no Iroquois raids that year but notes that the two tribes did join forces to hunt around the time of Kateri's birth.) Born in 1656, Tekakwitha was the couple's elder child. They later had a son.

Despite Tagaskouita's Christianity, neither child received baptism, as at this time there were no priests in the Iroquois villages. Other than the mother's pious Christianity, they were an ordinary Mohawk family. Then, in 1660, smallpox struck their village near Ossernenon, New York. The illness took Tekakwitha's mother, father, and little brother, and her uncle adopted her.

Although at her death her mother had fervently prayed that her daughter would remember the catechism she had learned, the girl's remembrance of—much less attachment to—her mother's Catholic faith was like an ember that would soon be extinguished. She was a normal Mohawk girl. She had good tribal manners and did not rebel against tribal customs. Her only distinguishing characteristic was her bad vision, a side effect of the smallpox. In fact, "Tekakwitha" means "She who bumps into things."

CHRISTIAN WITNESS

Sometime in her girlhood, the Onondaga Iroquois asked the French to send some Black Robes (Jesuits) to live at one of their villages. As with the Mohawks before them, the Onondagas wanted in on the fur trade. The Mohawks still did as well, and they resented the Onondagas' acquaintance with the Black Robes, especially given their hatred for Christianity. This helped bring an end to a fragile peace (and peace between the various Iroquois tribes and the French was always fragile).

When Tekakwitha was ten years old, the French burned her village Kanawaké in the middle of the night. They also did so to two other Mohawk towns. The Mohawks sued for peace. As part of the accord, the Jesuit superiors sent three priests to Kanawaké.

When these gentlemen arrived, the Mohawks couldn't believe they had come without an escort, especially considering all that had happened before. They respected the Jesuits for this display of courage. In a move that must have floored the newcomers, several Mohawk women asked for baptism. Tekakwitha, however, did not.

Though the welcome proved different from past experience, Iroquois behavior remained the same. One of the priests, a Fr. Pierron, had to witness cannibalism and the burning of the Mohicans' prisoners, including a newborn nursing from its mother. At least Father baptized the child before its premature death.

Fr. Pierron was a magnificent missionary, bold to the point of fool-hardiness. His goal, however, was that of Brébeuf: to force the Indians, out of honor, to let him live by their own code and traditions. The Indians began to change. For instance, they gave up worship of the god Areskoi when Father made that a condition of continued French friendship. And it wasn't lip service they gave him, these people who previous missionaries had said were so adept at lying. Father's words even "entered [the] heart" of the great Oneida Iroquois chief Garakontié, who converted.[26]

The next year, the Iroquois did something they never had before: They allowed the construction of a chapel at Kanawaké, to be staffed by Fr. Pierron's replacement, Fr. Boniface. Fr. Boniface became something like a pastor for the Mohawks, whereas previous Black Robes had been more like itinerant preachers.

The Iroquois first came to the chapel out of curiosity rather than any budding conviction. They especially liked the candle-festooned Nativity scene at Christmas (many had never seen candles), and the carols Father taught some converts transfixed them. Villagers began to convert, including a great warrior chief.

The Iroquois found the conversion of this chief unbelievable. His name was Kryn. His fervor for the faith proved authentic. When he asked if anyone would join him in moving to the Indian Christian village to the north, forty of Kanawaké's four hundred residents decided to join him.

Another person who converted was Mari Tsidouentes, formerly a raging alcoholic. So fierce was her resolve not to drink that when four men restrained her and tried to force brandy down her throat, she thrashed each one. Her zeal extended to other areas, too. If she found that the food at feasts came from pagan sacrifices, she would stand up, loudly denounce the whole affair, and storm back to her longhouse.

What was happening with Tekakwitha in these days? Nothing. Well, not nothing really. She did resolve not to marry. As far as we know, this had nothing to do with Christianity. Something kept her from marriage, but she didn't know what. Mohawk women did not remain single; they married. Something had to give.

In 1675, Fr. Jacques de Lamberville was assigned to Kanawaké. One day, on a whim, he peeked inside a longhouse, one where most of the residents hated the faith. Everyone was supposed to be out working, but the longhouse wasn't empty. Inside he found the nineteen-year-old Tekakwitha, who had injured her foot. The two began a conversation, a short one, and at its end, the maiden requested baptism.

Six months later, after giving sufficient instruction, Fr. de Lamberville granted Tekakwitha's request and gave her the baptismal name of Kateri, Mohawk for "Catherine." Many of the Mohawks rejoiced at the news, and for some reason they started calling her not *a* Christian but *the* Christian.

This soon became an epithet, however. Kateri refused to work on Sundays and holy days of obligation, so "Christian" became synonymous with "lazy person." Villagers decided that, since she would not work on Sundays, she would not eat on Sundays either. Considering that the Iroquois diet wasn't substantial to begin with, this was probably especially hard on Kateri.

Her fellow villagers also tried to paint her as a woman of loose virtue. That was untrue, of course, but in a village beset by intemperance, lust, and other deadly sins, her virtue and her rejection of vice stood in silent judgment of them. So they made her life very difficult.

One person who treated her well was the chief, her uncle, although his motivation wasn't religious tolerance. He wanted her to feel as though she had options other than fleeing to the Indian Christian village. Braves who had gone there simply to mock the residents ended up staying, as did those who went to rob what were, by Iroquois standards, huge stockpiles of food. With Kryn's having taken 10 percent of Kanawaké's population with him, Kateri's uncle couldn't afford to lose any more villagers.

A CALL TO KANAWAKA

The Indian village to which Kryn and the others had moved was called Kanawaka. It had not been intended as an Indian village, nor as a village at all. It started as a small chapel for those traveling to and from Montreal and for any Indians who might venture by.

However, an Oneida convert named Francis Tonsahoten, who likely had accepted Christ while a hostage among the Hurons, was asked to escort a Jesuit *donné* to Montreal. Francis brought his wife and five other Oneida braves with him for the job. For various reasons, the party had to winter at Kanawaka. Francis's wife and some of the other Indians had also visited Québec City. What they saw there of Christianity was enough for them to request baptism.

There was no return journey; the party stayed at Kanawaka (also known as Caughnawaga), where they could worship without fear of persecution by their fellow Indians. Within three years, twenty others joined them. Finally the Indians had a place where they could be wholly Christian and wholly Indian at the same time. The community was so attractive, twenty tribes were soon represented there.

The residents rebuilt the chapel, and its bells tolled the Angelus thrice a day. They insisted on moral living. Someone who became intoxicated had to spend the rest of the day in a pigsty. A more effective deterrent was public opinion. On the flip side was the villagers' charity.

Just as Kanawaka frightened her uncle and many others in Kanawaké, its flame drew Kateri's moth. You see, the French and Dutch had discovered that, instead of having to part with valuable goods such as muskets and cast iron kettles, they could ply Kanawaké's residents with liquor and get the same return in furs. The result: a lot of drunken Mohawks. Kateri's uncle saw how this disturbed his niece. He realized that she was a flight risk. He gave her an ultimatum: Choose between Christianity and life. That is how he phrased it. What she likely heard was: Choose between earthly death and eternal death. We know her decision.

One impediment to her escape was practical. How could she make the 250-mile journey, especially given that her uncle was an excellent tracker? Then one day, three lay Indian missionaries came to her village. They learned Kateri's uncle was signing a treaty with the Dutch at Fort Orange (today's Albany). After he left, the Christians made a dash for Kanawaka. What made the journey even more precarious was their need to purchase supplies at Fort Orange.

When the uncle returned and discovered Kateri's escape, he chased after her. He came so close to catching his niece that Kateri could see him walking down the path in front of her as she hid in some bushes. After several days he gave up the hunt.

Kateri was free.

When she arrived at Kanawaka, the priests convinced a woman named Anastasie to take in the newcomer. Anastasie had known Kateri's mother and lived in the same cabin as Kateri's adopted sister and brother-in-law.

Anastasie's influence on her was immediate. Kateri began to dress less frivolously. She attended two daily Masses. Her chores and duties, those ordinary things, she did in extraordinary ways. Her confessor saw her stop by the baptismal font each day to thank God for making her his child through the sacrament.

Kateri sprinkled her food with ashes as a mortification. She led people to gossip less by encouraging them to recount the lives of the saints instead of someone's faults. She also led people in singing for long periods of time.

Kateri spoke little of herself but much of Mary. Indeed, she had adopted a less vain appearance for love of Mary. She worked herself up to saying the rosary each day and eventually added the Litany of Loreto to her nighttime prayers. She never missed praying the Angelus.

GOD ALONE

Because of Kateri's lightning-like spiritual progress, the town priest invited her to make her First Communion on Christmas Day 1677. Very few Indians ever received Communion, certainly none who had been Christians for just half a year, so this was truly unprecedented.

Eventually, Kateri became friends with Marie Thérèse Tegaiagenta, a recovering alcoholic whom most people thought had shed a few too many brain cells along the way. What made Marie a good fit for Kateri was that both recognized their "desperate need for salvation." As Fr. Daniel Lowery, C.SS.R., has written, "It is easy to think of sin in abstract terms or even trivial terms. Only when we, like the saints, recognize the devastating power of sin in us, and our powerlessness to be set free from it, are we able to grasp in an experiential way the meaning of 'Savior.'"[27]

These women did not think of sin in abstract, trivial terms. It is said that the holier the saint, the greater their sensitivity to sin. Things those less dedicated to holiness find negligible are recognized by the holy for what they are: sin. So it was with these women. They appreciated the full meaning of the term *Savior*.

The two formed what was essentially a religious order, took on an additional member, and adopted for themselves a simple rule: None would ever marry. Again, Indians married—period. Therefore, marry Kateri must. Wasn't it best for her and the community?

The villagers tried several means to persuade our saint. Nothing succeeded. Still, feeling their pressure, she asked the priest his opinion. He suggested she think it over for three days. She left. Fifteen minutes later, she returned. She had thought and prayed over the matter for months. Three days, thirty days, what difference would it make?

Father blessed her decision. It had caused her no little confusion, second-guessing, and sadness. Now Kateri felt filled with joy.

Thus at 8:00 A.M. on the Feast of the Annunciation 1679, after morning Mass, Kateri became North America's first consecrated virgin. As if a light switch had been flipped, the other villagers fully accepted her new status. In her new role many began asking her for spiritual direction. Her advice was sound and merciful, and she proved a powerful intercessor. Our saint's persecution had ended.

THE END OF SUFFERING, THE BEGINNING OF LIFE

As Kateri entered her third winter at Kanawaka, she became severely ill. In winter, all but the eldest and youngest went hunting, which in lean years could take the party up to three hundred miles away. Thus she had no one to care for her. The best the remaining villagers could do was feed her and keep her hydrated and warm.

A Fr. Chauchetière frequently visited Kateri. He would tell her Christ's life story, using picture books to illustrate the lessons. She took such delight in this she invited the village children to these visits so they could hear the stories and see the pictures.

She grew ever weaker. On April 17, 1680, the Wednesday of Holy Week, at 3:00 P.M., the Hour of Mercy, Fr. Chauchetière saw Kateri's neck give a slight jolt. She had passed.

Why St. Kateri Tekakwitha Deserves Our Attention and Devotion

St. Kateri was not the always-holy, instant saint some have made her out to be. Instead she was like a lot of young people: She only gradually came to a faith in Christ. But when she did, wow!

If God wanted us to keep Sundays holy, by golly, Kateri wasn't going to work on Sundays. If Jesus wanted her to be a consecrated virgin, nothing would move her from that. This is what Jesus means when he tells us not to be lukewarm, when he challenges us, "Why do you call me 'Lord, Lord,' but do not do what I say"? (Luke 6:46).

Kateri's faith wasn't a self-medicating, comfortable "Let's get in the car and drive to Mass for our weekly dose of Catholicism." It cost her. She took seriously Jesus's words, "If any man would come after me, let him deny himself and take up his cross daily and follow me" (Luke 9:23).

Isn't this the sort of faith we all should seek to make our own?

Lord, being a Christian is the greatest privilege a person can have. Nevertheless, to live as a true Christian and thereby progress in holiness is hard, really hard. St. Kateri understood this. She didn't look for a featherbed when you handed her rough-grit sandpaper.

Please let her example help us persevere so we can reach her level of sanctity. And may her prayers on our behalf help us in this effort.

CHAPTER EIGHT

New Mexico

+ THE MOST DANGEROUS PLACE FOR A MISSIONARY TO BE +

Of all the dangerous mission fields in what is now the United States, none was more so than New Mexico. From 1542 through 1696, forty-six missionaries lost their lives in "The Land of Enchantment" (the state's nickname from Spanish times). Roughly half did so in the so-called Pueblo Revolt of 1680.

One wishes we could paint the Spanish colonists—particularly the lay Catholic and especially the conquistadores, who so proudly assumed the Christian mantle—as loving and understanding of the fact that all are created in God's image and thus possess innate human dignity. Sadly, nowhere in New Spain was that universally the case.[28]

Again, this was primarily a lay phenomenon. Although certainly not true across the board, many, many priests stalwartly and bravely loved and protected the Indians. That more natives weren't enslaved or massacred at will but rather received humane treatment is largely due to these brave and resolute men.

Many priests were also attuned enough to the native culture that they did not throw certain religious traditions out with the pagan bathwater. These missionaries either Christianized said customs or slowly phased them out once the natives converted.

A number of missionaries, however, had an "immediate, all-or-nothing" mentality. Among these were the missionaries who accompanied the first caravans of Spaniards that saddled into New Mexico in 1598. Lay and cleric alike had the idea that, within a short time, they would turn the Pueblo Indians into Spaniards. Not surprisingly, the Pueblo had different ideas. While many eventually came to the missions as sincere Christians, most came simply because the Spanish would defend them against attacks by the Navajo and Apache.

The savagery of the Navajo and Apache nations must have been tremendous if the Pueblo decided to trust the colonists. After all, in a 1599 battle at Acoma Pueblo, the Spanish killed a thousand Indians and captured five hundred, many of whom promptly became slaves. This was despite slavery's illegality under both imperial and Church law. Two years later, another battle at Quarai resulted in nine hundred dead and two hundred captured.

The settlers demanded from the Pueblo land, food, work (because that was beneath them), everything that was not bolted down (including blankets during the winter), and conversion. The Pueblo did get something in return—for instance, more food, as the Spanish gave them new crops and taught them better farming methods and animal husbandry. As already noted, the Spanish provided a defense against their enemies.

However, given what the Pueblo had to endure, the ledger wasn't balanced. The Spaniards felt little obligation to these obviously inferior beings. Faced with various firearms and artillery against their spears and arrows, the Pueblo settled down under a humiliating yoke.

Then there were the Franciscans, who were like the proverbial bull in a china shop. The friars burned the Pueblos' ceremonial places and destroyed their religious objects, not recognizing the Pueblo religion as an intrinsic part of these people who would rather die than give up their beliefs. Needless to say, these priests didn't see many come into the fold.

Yet even those critical of the Spanish admit there were brave, good, and loving friars who ventured unaccompanied to isolated Pueblos to evangelize and serve. These men truly showed Christ's love, and the stories they told of salvation history resonated in the ears of the Pueblo, who were storytellers themselves. A few conversions did result from these men's efforts, even though some natives continued to secretly practice their traditions. It was the converts who built their pueblo churches, true, but theirs was not the labor of slaves. Rather, it was lovingly and pridefully rendered.

This was the exception, however. Various factors worked together to decimate the Pueblo population, taking it from roughly thirty thousand in 1598 to seventeen thousand by 1680. Rather than extend them a helping hand, both lay and clerical Spaniards argued over who had a better right to the Indians' goods and labors. Thus the overall effect of Spanish domination became that of a pressure cooker turned up too high, and the natives revolted. The first rebellion happened in 1632, followed by another in 1650. The colonists easily put these down.

One can understand why the Spaniards' hypocrisy enraged the Pueblos, especially the converts. Hadn't the friars taught them they were all brethren in Christ? Weren't all Christians called to love and serve one another? Disillusioned, many reverted to paganism. Even those who didn't apostatize joined their voices to the chorus of revolution being composed in their midst. The man who became its conductor was a shaman named Popay. Today his statue stands in Congress's Statuary Hall for his role as leader of an inexcusable massacre.

Amassing an army of eight thousand mostly Christian soldiers, the Pueblo struck early on August 10, 1680, the Feast of St. Lawrence. First they struck the churches (Fr. Juan de Pío became the protomartyr of this offensive), then farms and villages, killing everyone who couldn't hide. The roughly 250 dead included around forty-five Indians who would not renounce their faith and join the rebellion.

Many more Spaniards would have died if not for their leader's determination to go on the offensive, "until dying or conquering." He told everyone that the best "armor" was to redouble one's prayers, "to appease the divine wrath," and he ordered the mission's three priests to say Mass. Then he exhorted "all alike to repentance for their sins" and asked the priests "to absolve us from guilt and punishment."[29] The ensuing sally proved highly successful and lifted the siege.

Why the Martyrs of New Mexico Deserve Our Attention and Devotion
The Church has never encouraged forced conversion, yet that is arguably what Christians attempted with the Pueblo. As 1 Corinthians 12:11 tells us, the Holy Spirit works where he wills. He converts. We do our part and leave the rest up to him.

Lord, give us the humility to know that you, not we, are responsible for converting people. Use us as conduits who are ever mindful of your sovereignty. Through the New Mexican martyrs' prayers, help us bring many souls to you.

CHAPTER NINE

Fr. Gabriel de la Ribourde, O.F.M., Rec.

+ Killed by the Kickapoo +

Let's take a trip, at least in our minds.

Buy an airplane ticket for Makhachkala, Dagestan. Bring with you nothing but some changes of clothing and some necessary books—namely, a Bible, a catechism, and a good Kumyk-English dictionary. In Dagestan few speak English, 98 percent of the population professes Islam, and the culture is radically different from that of North America.

In 2010, suspected Islamic militants murdered a Protestant pastor outside his church for the "crime" of converting Muslims. Radical Salafist Muslims attack their coreligionists for being heretics. Indeed, violence in this Russian republic is far from uncommon. Oh, and hardly any Catholics live here. In fact, authorities shuttered the one registered parish.

Your mission: Bring souls to Christ.

Sound inviting? Now you know how the missionaries coming to North America must have felt, because they faced the same sort of situation. Furthermore, most not only volunteered for mission work, they also recognized the likelihood of martyrdom. Indeed, every religious order that sent evangelists to this continent has its share of martyrs, including the little known Récollet Franciscans. That brings us to the story of Fr. Gabriel de la Ribourde.

Born in Burgundy, France, in 1610, and last in the line of his noble family, Gabriel renounced his family fortune and entered the Récollets on All Saints' Day, November 1, 1638. After ordination he spent much of the next thirty years as superior and director of novices of the monastery at Béthune, Pas-de-Calais. Then he transferred to Canada, where he shortly became his order's superior in New France.

Fr. de la Ribourde also served as a missionary at various outposts and forts in French territory. Specifically, he joined Robert de la Salle's expedition to Illinois as chaplain. They ended up at Fort St. Louis, which was situated atop Starved Rock, in what is now Illinois's Starved Rock State Park. Fr. de la Ribourde was evidently well liked by the Illini. Their chief, Asapista, adopted him, and the two spent a lot of time hunting together.

In the end, however, Father and a mission companion had very few converts to show for their efforts. It was judged that, for these indigenous, the faith was just too much outside their worldview. Further hampering their efforts was Father's great difficulty with the language. As a result, baptisms amounted to a handful of dying babies and two or three adults.

When the Iroquois attacked their Illini hosts, the Indians fled, leaving Ribourde behind. He and two other priests took an ill-provisioned canoe and tried to reach Green Bay via the Illinois River. On September 19, 1680, during a stop on a riverbank to fix their leaky craft, Father decided to pray his breviary in the shade of some woods, for it was hot. At some point Kickapoo Indians attacked and killed him. As dusk fell, his companions went looking for him and found his corpse naked and scalped.

Why Fr. Gabriel de la Ribourde Deserves Our Attention and Devotion
As a young man with money and connections, Fr. de la Ribourde could have done anything. Instead he gave away everything to serve God. At roughly age sixty (at a time when life expectancy was thirty-five

years), he left his thirty-year career in France for missionary work, since that is what God, through his superiors, wanted from him. Alone in the wilderness, bad at speaking the local language, he didn't let these obstacles keep him from working hard to save souls. To top it all off, one day, the seventy-year-old simply wanted to pray and get out of the hot sun, and that led to his death. Sheesh, talk about hard knocks!

Yet, Father simply did what his Master expected which is to put Jesus before everything else (see Luke 9:62 and Matthew 10:37). He and others like him held nothing back from God. That helped lay the foundation for what made North America great.

Do we do the same? If not, how can we give God more?

Father God, our hope and our end, help us hold nothing back in loving you. Help us give and not count the price. Teach us to always rejoice in serving you, even when it costs us. This is a hard prayer to pray, Lord, but we trust you because of your totally self-sacrificing love for us.

CHAPTER TEN

Ann "Goody" Glover

+ The Witch Who Wasn't +

Practically everyone has heard of the Salem witch trials in 1692. Authorities falsely accused twenty-eight people in this Massachusetts village. Twenty-four were executed or died in jail. What many people do not know is that this famous episode in New England's colonial past had its precursor in the unfortunate demise of several people in Boston, especially an illiterate Catholic washerwoman.

The story begins in Ireland with Oliver Cromwell's three-year conquest of that land in the mid-seventeenth century. Cromwell led the Puritan army during England's Civil War (1642–1651) and helped it defeat the royalists. In 1649, the new government chose him to put down an Irish rebellion, which he did, in part by killing between two hundred thousand and six hundred thousand civilians.

Afterward Cromwell sold thirty thousand Irish into slavery, most of whom ended up in Montserrat, Jamaica, or Barbados. Although we think slavery in the Americas was strictly a black or even Indian phenomenon, the fact is that Irish slaves accounted for a huge percentage of bondsmen under Britain's colonial rule. True, Irish slavery didn't begin with Cromwell, nor did it end with him. Still, he sent so many Irish to Montserrat that Gaelic was the island's official language until the early 1800s.

In any event, two who came to Barbados in this fashion were Ann Glover and her husband, whose name has been lost. Ann later claimed that shortly after their daughter Mary's birth, the British killed her husband for refusing to give up his Catholic faith.

She and Mary came to Boston, probably around 1680 in the large wave of Indian and Irish slaves who were imported by the Puritans. One slave dealer was Rev. Samuel Parris, a Puritan minister in Salem who would figure prominently in that town's witch trials.

At some point Ann gained her freedom, and she became a washerwoman with several clients, some of whom she also served as a nanny. Most of the young city's residents, however, did not want to employ anyone with her papist inclinations. The Glovers were probably the only Catholics in Boston. People threw stones at them, proselytized them to the point of harassment, and cursed them. Others utterly shunned them.

As a result, work was hard to find and pay only grudgingly given. The small family barely scraped by. If not for the kindness of Robert Calef, a prominent Baptist merchant (Baptists were also persecuted by the Puritan majority), and later a Mrs. Nourse from Salem, the two would have starved.

Among the few families to employ them were the Goodwins. Ann and Mary washed their clothes and looked after their four children. The Goodwins attended Old North Church (not the one made famous by Paul Revere's ride, which didn't exist at the time), and Rev. Cotton Mather was their pastor.

One day in 1687, thirteen-year-old Martha Goodwin and twelve-year-old Mary got into an argument after Martha accused Ann of stealing some of her family's clothes.[30] Mary rose to her mother's defense and accused Martha of simply trying to get Ann in trouble. She shouted at Martha, "You may have us whipped, but to the sermons we will not go."

Neither Mary nor Ann protested innocence in the theft. Instead Mary referred to "sermons." We can conclude that she thought Martha was simply making another attempt at blackmailing them into becoming Protestants. For the townspeople would have seen the Glovers' attendance at Protestant services as an accommodation to the majority, if not an outright victory for it. But the Glovers would not compromise their Catholic faith.

This altercation appears to have led Martha to harbor spite and possibly some degree of revenge in her heart. A short time later, maybe even that day, she had such a hysterical fit that her stonemason father, John, rushed to Rev. Mather's home. He in turn brought in several physicians, all of whom remarked that the girl's wildness had a diabolical origin. By 1688, the other three Goodwin offspring exhibited the same behaviors.

Certainly the contortions of Martha and her siblings as reported by Mather would have frightened anyone. He wrote that the children's "Tongues would be drawn down their Throats; another-while they would be pull'd out upon their Chins, to a prodigious length. They would have their Mouths opened unto such a Wideness, that their Jaws went out of joint; and anon they would clap together again with a Force like that of a strong Spring-Lock."[31]

However, consider the fact that the supposed victims of the "witches" in the Salem trial manifested almost identical behaviors. And in 1706 Ann Putnam, Jr., one of Salem's principal accusers of alleged witches, recanted and apologized for her role in sending innocent people to their deaths fourteen years before.

Also, Dijon quotes several contemporary English preachers to show that being a papist and a witch were seen as indistinguishable. Indeed, Glover, Mather wrote, was "a scandalous old Irish Woman in the neighbourhood."[32] Dijon says Mather also called her "very poor, a Roman Catholick and obstinate in idolatry."[33] Another historian writes: "John Goodwin…began to ascribe the sudden fits of his children to the 'Papistical teaching' of the old Irish laundress and her daughter, and brought the case to Cotton Mather."[34]

Eventually authorities searched the laundress's home, where they found "secret" images, including a crucifix and some stuffed dolls—maybe substitutes for statues of saints. Most historians believe these objects had religious significance.

Wrote Mather, "The Magistrates being awakened by the Noise of these Grievous and Horrid Occurrences, examined [Ann Glover]… under the suspicion of having employ'd these Troublesome Demons, and she gave such a Wretched Account of herself, that she was committed unto the Gaoler's Custody."[35] Ann's widowhood didn't help, as widows were more often accused of witchery.[36]

Ann was imprisoned sometime before August 4, 1688, and she languished in chains through mid-November, enduring what must have been relentless questioning. Making matters worse, back then jailers provided the imprisoned no food. Just as Ann and Mary, who went into the gaol with her mother, relied on Robert Calef and Mrs. Nourse for food when they were free, so now they relied on them during their imprisonment.

Under such withering pressures, Mather writes that Ann Glover admitted to witchcraft. Why did he not release her then? Puritan law said that anyone who confessed sorcery earned freedom.[37] If witchcraft truly was the issue, Mather and the magistrates should not have continued to hold her. Why did similar forced confessions given by alleged witches in Salem enable those non-Catholic people to escape execution, even though the confessions were wholly self-serving?

Another episode in English history possibly sheds light on the situation. After the expulsion of the Cromwellians from power, Charles I's son Charles II became king. Upon his death in 1685, his brother James II ascended to the throne. James had converted to Catholicism, and within three years, his support had all but evaporated. A group of nobles, most of them former followers and close counselors, mobilized behind His Majesty's son-in-law, Prince William of Orange. In June 1688, James lost his crown in what the Protestants called the Glorious Revolution, "glorious" because no "stain" of "popery" now touched the throne.

How may this have played a role in the Glover case? In 1686, James II appointed Edmund Andros as governor of New England. Upon his arrival Andros, an Anglican, requested a church in which to hold services. When the Puritans rebuffed this request, he confiscated one from them.

Although very different from the Mass, the Anglican service was more like the Catholic liturgy than anything the Puritans did. So the fact that a Catholic king had appointed a heavy-handed Anglican who readily made enemies as head of an overwhelmingly Puritan colony made Andros's position somewhat precarious. He had enough troubles of his own. While some think he recognized Ann's innocence, doing anything to help her might have risked his position.[38]

In any event, on November 15, 1688, four months after William became king, Ann Glover's case finally went to trial. Because witchcraft suspects had no right to counsel, this "despised, crazy, ill-conditioned old woman, an Irish Roman Catholic,"[39] had to defend herself. Arrayed against her were some of Boston's best minds. She had trouble understanding their questions and making herself understood. She could only answer in Gaelic, for though she understood some English, she couldn't speak it. It could not have helped her case that the Goodwin children would scream in agony every time she opened her mouth.

Prosecutors asked Ann to recite the Lord's Prayer, for it was thought that none who consorted with Satan could do so. She delivered the prayer in Irish just fine. None, however, could understand that tongue, so they asked if she could pray it in Latin. She could, but she mispronounced a few words, which is to be expected of someone "whose memory was confused by age."[40]

Ann could not say the prayer in English. Furthermore, she would not say it with the concluding phrase that, until the Second Vatican Council, no Catholic would use, namely, "For thine is the kingdom, the power, and the glory..." Mather reported, "She could not end it."[41] For this they judged her to be in league with the devil.

Robert Calef reports, "It may appear that the generality of her answers were nonsense, and her behavior like that of one distracted. Yet the doctors, finding her as she had been for many years, brought her *in compos mentis*; and setting aside her crazy answers to some ensnaring questions, the proof against her was wholly deficient. The jury brought her in guilty."

The night of the conviction, Mather visited Ann in her cell and harassed her with more questions. In leaving her, he asked if she would like his prayers. If prayers would help, she responded, she would pray for herself. In other words, "Buzz off, creep."[42]

The next day, the gaolers and Mather led Ann to the hangman's scaffold, which as Providence would have it, sat directly under what would one day be Boston cathedral's holy water font. Along the way people taunted the bedraggled woman. One historian quotes a contemporary source:

There was a great concourse of people to see if the Papist would relent.... Before her executioners she was bold and impudent, making to forgive her accusers and those who put her off. She predicted that her death would not relieve the children, saying that it was not she that afflicted them.[43]

It is also said that among her last words were these: "I die a Catholic."[44] As the hangman dropped the platform from under her feet, Ann held a crucifix to her chest.

Mary Glover died a raving lunatic the following spring. The Goodwin children, it will be noted, continued manifesting odd behavior after Ann's death, just as she had predicted.

Why Ann Glover Deserves Our Attention and Devotion

Ann was a victim of bigots who were technically part of the same body of Christ as she. Her story reminds us of the need to pray for comity, peace, and the unification of all peoples in God's holy Church.

Lord, you said we could expect others to hate us because of you. What you didn't say was that this could happen with those who also profess your holy name. If you ever allow us to face persecution and false accusations at the hands of our separated brethren, help us to bear these with the same grace and fortitude Ann Glover exhibited.

CHAPTER ELEVEN

Fr. Juan de Parga, O.F.M., and Br. Marcos Delgado, O.F.M.

+ DEATH AMONGST THE APALACHEE +

The last Catholic martyrs in Florida—scores of Spanish and Indian Catholics—died in what we now call the Apalachee massacre. The Franciscan missionaries Fr. Juan de Parga and Br. Marcos Delgado are at the core of this story, which isn't to deny the tragedy of the many Apalachees who suffered martyrdom, torture, and enslavement.

It was 1704. In 1701 Spain's King Carlos II had died, setting off a war of succession that engulfed Spain, France, and Germany. Britain took the opportunity of France and Spain fighting one another to press its claims and capture territories in the New World, resulting in Queen Anne's War.

As part of this effort, former South Carolina Governor James Moore launched a raid on the Spanish missions along the Florida panhandle. The goal was to weaken the Spaniards and capture slaves to fund the venture. His efforts were successful beyond his wildest dreams.

Moore reduced the three towns on St. Mark's Island to ashes and killed all their Christian inhabitants. A brief skirmish next took place at Mission Patali. Its chaplain, Fr. Juan de Parga, exhorted his Indian converts to fight bravely for their lives, their homes, and their holy faith. The battle, however, was hopeless from the start.

The campaign's only significant fighting took place at Mission Ayubale on January 25, 1704. There Fr. Ángel Miranda led a determined resistance for nine hours against the roughly sixty English and

Creek Indians. The mixed Spanish-Indian force of twenty-nine men only surrendered when they had no more arrows.

As soon as the skirmish ended, Moore had a stake erected and Fr. de Parga tied to it, then watched while the man burned to death.[45] Not believing his eyes, Br. Manuel Delgado bravely rushed toward the flames to free his friend. For his effort, a British sword cut him down.

The Englishman then gave Ayubale's military commander, Lt. Mejia, an outrageously high ransom demand that the captives had no hope of paying. On January 31, when this became clear, Moore had Fr. Ángel, Lt. Mejia, some soldiers, and many converts share in Parga's fate.[46]

The majority of the Apalachee Christians were sold into slavery. Some escaped, however, to the French colony at Mobile, Alabama, where they set up a village just north of the city.

Why Fr. Juan de Parga and Br. Marcos Delgado Deserve Our Attention and Devotion

Recall from chapter two that Florida had not been the site of any fruitful ministry for missionaries. Yet these men ventured into this territory, converted many natives to the faith, and then gave their lives to stand with them against British atrocities. Truly they are great witnesses.

Br. Marcos is a great example of a faithful friend. He gave his life in an effort to save his colleague. "Greater love has no man than this, that a man lay down his life for his friends" (John 15:13).

Lord, may there be no envy, greed, or unseemly competition among fellow Christians but only charity, encouragement, and prayer for one another. In your name we pray with confidence, for you are the source of all love in the Body of Christ.

CHAPTER TWELVE

Fr. Sébastien Râle

+ THE MAMA BEAR FATHER +

Sébastien Râle was born in Pontarlier, Franche-Comte, France, in 1657. His parents did not want him to join the Jesuits, but he felt he could not turn his back on his true Father. After teaching for a short time, he volunteered for the missions and came to North America in 1689, roughly forty years after the death of St. Isaac Jogues. The thirty-two-year-old priest arrived in New France as the quintessential French missionary: proudly patriotic, pious, and badly wanting to bring people to Christ.

After spending some time among the Wabanaki in what is today Norridgewock, Maine, Fr. Râle was sent to the Illini beyond Lake Michigan. War between the French and British reached the New World in 1694, and that is when his superiors sent Father back to the Wabanaki.

This people was ready for what Father had to give them. Fr. William Clark, a professor of religious studies, says that by the early seventeenth century, changes that had happened since the white man's arrival had left the Wabanaki spiritually unmoored.[47] Thus this mission provided fertile soil for evangelization, and by 1698, Fr. Râle had enough converts to build a church. Indeed, because of this man, the Wabanaki became a Catholic tribe.

The tribe loved their priest. He loved them. He brought them a Savior and the sacraments. He cared for them in a tender way. He treated them as equals, not as animals as the English did. He fell in love with their simple and yet almost mystical way of seeing the world. They taught him something every day.

Fr. Râle celebrated the sacred liturgy every morning, at which the natives served. Benediction followed Sunday Mass in the chapel that Father, an artist, had beautifully decorated. He held public vespers every night. He also created prayers and a catechism in Wabanaki. He would lead up to forty respected village men, each dressed in cassock and surplice, in village Eucharistic processions.

Like most indigenous at the time, the Wabanaki maintained a highly mobile annual schedule, going here in the spring, there in the summer, and so on. Whenever Father accompanied them on these sojourns, and it was often, he brought his Mass kit. His flock wanted the sacraments.

With the eruption of Queen Anne's War in North America in 1702, English and French colonial forces fought once again. Although the English governor of Massachusetts asked the Wabanaki not to, the tribe wholeheartedly threw its lot in with the French. Who could have provoked the natives against the English in such a way? Why, it couldn't have been anything the British had done—besides malign Catholicism and try to take Wabanaki land. Comparing their priest and his kindness with British treatment, is it any wonder that the Wabanaki chose the French side? But French prejudice toward the British also played its part.

The British, however, laid sole blame for the Indians' bad attitude toward them with Fr. Râle, and so they put a bounty on his head. In 1705, during a cold winter, a force of 275 soldiers marched on Norridgewock. Though Father fled, the English torched the town, including its church. Five years later, everything had been rebuilt.

In 1713 the Treaty of Utrecht ended Queen Anne's War, and one of its conditions was that the Indians become British subjects. That wouldn't work. First, the Wabanaki detested the English. Second, they didn't consider themselves French subjects. They were an independent nation. Furthermore, English laws outlawed Catholic clergy and thus the effective practice of their religion.

Again, the British thought that the Wabanaki had allied themselves with the French only because of Râle. If he didn't keep stoking their fears against them, the Indians would gladly switch sides. No. The Wabanaki allied with the French because the French were Catholic and let them have their religion.

But while he was no friend of the British, Fr. Râle didn't protect French claims to the Wabanaki either. He protected Wabanaki claims to their land and their rights. The British—and the French—could not comprehend this. Tensions, therefore, continued.

In 1721, Fr. Râle led 250 Indians under a French flag in a peaceful raid on the British village of Georgetown. Peaceful, yet with a message: "This is our land. Get out." In response, the British attacked Norridgewock six months later. Father escaped once more.

Later that year, in June 1722, the Wabanakis retaliated for the attack on their village by burning Brunswick and even taking colonists' lives in unmerciful ways.

Râle knew what the British would do in response, especially after Massachusetts issued a declaration of war in 1722. He urged all who would to leave Maine for New France. The Wabanakis told him to leave as well, but he would not desert those who wanted to stay.

The British finally retaliated in August 1724, when over two hundred English soldiers stealthily sailed up the Kennebec and laid a surprise siege on Norridgewock. This time Fr. Râle purposefully did not escape. Instead, he stood underneath a huge cross in the town's center and drew the offenders' attention so others could flee. Over twenty natives died with him. The English publicly displayed his scalp in Boston.

Fr. Sébastien's execution came at the end of roughly thirty years of total devotion to and love for the Wabanaki. He had written his nephew shortly before his death, "As for what concerns me personally I assure you, that I see, that I hear, that I speak, only as a [sauvage]."[48]

While no entity has officially entered Fr. Râle's cause for canonization, many refer to him as "venerable," much as Europeans refer to their local faithfully departed as "blessed" or "saint," even though it is simply local custom and has no official approval.

Why Fr. Sébastien Râle Deserves Our Attention and Devotion

Biographers make it clear that, from the moment he entered the New World, Father wanted to love those whom God had called him to evangelize. We see this in the extraordinary lengths to which he went in order to become fluent in the Wabanaki tongue and how he accepted them where they were in their spiritual life, not where an eighteenth-century European mind-set might want them to be. This bonded him with the Wabanaki and enabled him to faithfully serve and protect his tribe for three decades.

The New Evangelization similarly calls us to take people where they are, not where we wish they were, to learn their "language," and to show them unrelenting love while not shirking from defining sin for what it is. This strategy is as old as St. Paul. By following it, we will bind people to Christ in a way that events and the world can never break.

Jesus, you called us to make disciples of all nations. Today we see that even the people of our own nation, not just those of foreign lands, need conversion.

First let us convert our own hearts, so that we may fittingly proclaim the Gospel. Then fill us with the Holy Spirit, so that we may imitate Fr. Sébastien and help others find salvation in you. We ask this in your name.

CHAPTER THIRTEEN

Fr. Luís Jayme, O.F.M.

+ THAT AIN'T NO WAY TO TREAT YOUR PADRE, NO WAY +

Born October 18, 1740, at a farm in the village of Sant Joan on the Spanish Mediterranean island of Majorca, and given the name Melchor Jayme, our next subject was smart, and so his pastor educated the peasant boy until he turned fifteen. That is when his father brought him to the Convent School of San Bernadino in the city of Petra, Majorca. Bl. Junípero Serra was an alumnus of that school, and he also hailed from the town. As for Majorca in general, so many Franciscan missionaries to California came from the island that some have called it the state's spiritual godmother.

Just before his twentieth birthday, Melchor joined the Franciscans, who gave him the name Luís and sent him to the Convento de San Francisco seminary, another alma mater of Fr. Serra. After completion of his studies and ordination, Fr. Jayme taught philosophy at San Francisco for five years, until 1770. Then the Franciscans transferred him to the California missions and made San Diego de Alcalá his first assignment. Of course, Father had to learn the local language, but he proved so adept at this, he even wrote a catechism in that tongue.

As we saw in the story about the Virginia martyrs, the *conquistadores'* bad example often hindered the missionaries' evangelization efforts. Well, Mission San Diego was right next to the soldiers' *presidio* (or fortress). One reason for placing missions and presidios near one another was to protect the missionaries in case the indigenous revolted. Yet Fr. Jayme wrote Fr. Junípero Serra that as long as this proximity existed, the mission would not thrive. He was willing to take the risk of being unprotected in order to spread the Gospel.

Furthermore, the water supply at that location proved unreliable. This threatened crops and thus presented the risk of famine. Father obtained permission to move to an eastward valley a few miles away.

The move to Nipaguay, the valley's Indian name, paid off, for soon the number of indigenous wanting baptism grew, and by the year of his martyrdom, Father could count 431 local Christians. Furthermore, exactly one month before he died, he and his vicar baptized sixty souls. He might have had even more baptisms, as he notes in a letter to Fr. Serra, but since "we could not give them *atole* [a dish] every time they appeared, the quantity of corn being already very small, they stopped coming."[49]

Still, while the missions were by and large very good, the friars ran them with an overly paternalistic attitude. Indeed, in Fr. Serra's writings he refers to the friars as parents and the Indians as children who occasionally needed corporal punishment. One can see the problems this might have posed for native adults, not the least of which was that spanking and the like were totally unknown in their culture. Also, the Franciscans did not trust their converts to be around the unconverted, because in their experience it often led to backsliding or worse. Therefore, if you were an Indian, once you checked into the mission, you could never leave.

It is for these and several other reasons that, on November 4, 1775, shortly after midnight, six hundred natives from the surrounding countryside—led by two recently escaped apostates—snuck into the mission. Their goal? To slay the few soldiers who had been dispatched from the presidio to stand guard and then kill the priests. And why? Because the priests wanted to convert all to Christ.

First the Indians raided the mission, stealing whatever was valuable and not nailed down, especially in the chapel. After that they consigned the whole complex to flames. By this time the place was a nightmarish, swirling mix of human panic and the attackers' bloodlust.

While he could have joined others in the militarily secure part of the compound, Fr. Jayme instead walked toward the frenzied Indians, giving them his customary and pious salutation. Whether this caused the Indians to hesitate or stoked their fiery fury to even greater intensity, we don't know. What we do know is that they took Father, savagely beat and stripped him, and then rained down on his body arrows and large stones until his life drained away.

The next morning survivors found the priest's naked body near a stream. His attackers had so disfigured him that only the white flesh of his consecrated hands was recognizable. This God had seen fit to preserve untouched.

When apprised of the tragedy, Bl. Junípero responded, "Thanks be to God; now that the terrain has been watered by blood, the conversion of the San Diego Indians will take place."[50] And it did. A little more than two generations later, the number of baptisms had grown to 6,638.

Why Fr. Luís Jayme Deserves Our Attention and Devotion
What is the one thing Fr. Jayme never did? He never acted on his own behalf. Everything he did was for others and a greater good. All was a total act of self-donation. That's not easy to do, is it? If it was, we wouldn't find it so awe inspiring.

Yet we are all called to do this, which is partly what it means to "be perfect, as your heavenly Father is perfect" (Matthew 5:48). If we do this, none of us will need martyrdom to become saints. Furthermore, we will radically change the world.

Holy Spirit, thank you for inspiring Fr. Luís Jayme's total self-abandonment. Help us follow his example in all we do and with everyone we meet, so that when our race is run, we will hear those words all long to hear, "Well done, good and faithful servant" (Matthew 25:23).

The Eighteenth and Nineteenth Centuries

The late eighteenth century and all the 1800s are marked by both the least and the most martyrdoms on North American soil. What? How can both be true?

During this time period we have the smallest number of *named* North Americans who lost their lives because of their Catholicism. Yet this was the period most beset by sectarian strife, in which many *nameless* folk died at least in part because of their Catholicism.

This age gave birth to the Know-Nothing Party and the "Native" (that is, nonimmigrant) movement in the United States. It produced scads of books full of the most lurid stories about what *really* happened in convents and monasteries. If half the stories featured in these penny "exposés" were actually true, it would make the abuse scandals of our own time look almost tame by comparison. All of this propaganda did much to stoke anti-Catholic prejudice on both sides of the St. Lawrence River.

After the British took over Canada in the late eighteenth century, the "tolerance" for which the dominion is so famous effectively stopped, then as now, at the door of the Catholic Church. For instance, around 1812 Governor General James Craig tried to force Canadian Catholics into a sort of Anglicanized Catholic Church. However, this effort failed. War was once again the reason.

The War of 1812 was in full swing, and the Americans had invaded Canada. Would it really pay to have nearly a quarter million of the dominion's inhabitants galvanized into becoming enemy sympathizers? In return for their unrelenting support, the government left the Church and its members unmolested.

This isn't to say that Canadian Catholics experienced no violence. For instance, every year on July 12, various communities held the Burgoyne Day parade. It was always a time for heightened anti-Catholic bigotry and possible violence due to the refusal of Catholics to lie down in the face of blatant prejudice. July 12, you see, was the anniversary of the Battle of the River Boyne. Fought on Ireland's east coast in 1690, it proved the decisive battle between Catholic James II and Protestant William of Orange. As such, July 12 was often a day on which one could expect trouble between Protestants and Catholics.

The "trouble" was highly ritualized. The Orangemen (the Protestants) would march on the papist side of town. Each side would trade insults. There might even be some fisticuffs or a melee. However, both sides went home after a while, each content with having shown the heretics just what it meant to be a true Christian. No one got really hurt.

That wasn't the case in 1849, though. In what became known as the Battle of Slabtown in today's St. Catharines, Ontario, Irish Catholics prepared to meet the expected Protestant demonstrators—who never showed. Befuddled, the Catholics marched to the Orange part of town and stood outside the dinner hall where the Orangemen were commemorating the anniversary with a meal. After unsuccessfully challenging their opponents to come out, the Catholics prepared to leave but first let out three cheers—one for Queen Victoria, one for the governor, and one for the pope.

It was one thing for those bloody papists to cry out for queen and governor. That the Protestants could tolerate. But cheering for the *pope?* That was too much.

And so some of the Orangemen appeared, brandishing guns. These they fired, wounding four and killing two. One of the dead was an impoverished husband and father who hadn't wanted to come but whose staying at home would have cost him his job. Yet his coming cost him his life. Still, on that day in July, it wasn't just that one man who should have stayed at home—it was all of them.

In the United States, the attitude toward Catholics was similar to that in Canada.

Following the Revolution, the religious liberty situation in the thirteen colonies hadn't much improved. In 1784, Bishop John Carroll wrote the papal nuncio at Paris that their co-religionists could only cautiously practice their faith lest they give the majority a reason to take away their rights, so deeply rooted was America's anti-Catholicism.

Rather than give in to this situation, many headed west for Bardstown, Kentucky (including this writer's ancestors, who had once been English recusants). A small town even then, Bardstown thus became one of this nation's first dioceses. Eventually Nativist (that is, anti-Catholic) pressure pushed many of the faithful to places such as Perryville, Missouri; Vincennes, Indiana; Charleston, South Carolina; and even Québec. Imagine pulling up everything for your religion. Yet if Catholics couldn't practice their faith, what good would possessing the world do for them?

In 1831, anti-Catholicism led to the destruction of New York City's St. Mary Church. During the night of August 9, 1834, a mob looted and burned down a Boston-area convent and its boarding school; despite several trials featuring eyewitness testimony, no one was ever convicted for this crime. In 1844 Philadelphia riots saw two churches and the houses of Irishmen burned and their residents perish. The proximate cause for this was Catholics' refusal to let schools force their children to read the Protestant translation of the Bible. Nor did parents want them compelled to say the Protestant version of the Our Father.

Anti-Catholic sentiment culminated in the founding of the Know-Nothings (c. 1852–1860), a political party whose primary platform plank was anti-Catholicism. At one point it had enough power to control several large cities' governments, some governorships, entire state legislatures, and many seats in Congress.

Anti-papist prejudice wasn't the only reason for hostility to the faith. There were also economic and social factors. In words we hear echoed today, many exclaimed, "They're stealing jobs from native-born Americans!" Such cries arose out of the fact that, by 1850, one-seventh of all U.S. residents were immigrants. (As a percentage, today's undocumented immigrant population is a quarter of that.) Immigrants were flooding U.S. borders, thus straining a job market already tight due to successive economic downturns. Some Catholics were becoming professionally successful. This also threatened the established order, because success begets power.

The anxiety caused by the influx of migrants continued to express itself in violence. In a September 1854 attack in Newark, New Jersey, an Irish bystander named McCarty was shot and killed. Then in Louisville, Kentucky, on August 5, 1855, the night before Election Day, Know-Nothings created a hellish inferno out of Irish and German immigrants' row houses. This was a remarkably effective way of suppressing the Catholic vote. Besides the intimidation the arson caused, two Micks could not vote (being lynched'll do that to ya), several more died inside their burning homes, and others were shot dead as they fled the fires. All told, almost one hundred people died by flame or gunshot.

Another compelling story is that of Duffy's Cut.

In the early summer of 1832, a Pennsylvania railroad contractor and Irishman named Phil Duffy hired fifty-seven impoverished Irish immigrants whose average age was twenty-two. Their job? To lay Philadelphia's famous Main Line railroad. The work, which earned the all-Catholic group twenty-five cents per day ($5.66 in today's U.S. dollars), took place in a heavily wooded forest amid steep hills. These were not only littered by large rocks but often liberally adorned with brambles, briars, and poison oak.

By late August, all the men had died.

A few of the men had contracted cholera because of the labor camp's unsanitary conditions. Rather than quarantine those persons and get them adequate medical care (which existed even back then), Duffy and a local vigilante organization quarantined all the workers in a thirty-square-foot pen.

Why would Duffy treat his fellow countrymen in this way? Immaculata University history professor Dr. Bill Watson says, "Duffy cared only about getting the work done on time, and the men's death was merely an inconvenience to him."[51] At the time American citizens took the same view of the Irish that many today take of low-skilled Hispanic immigrants, and for much the same reasons: They were Catholic, had too many kids, and were illiterate, unwashed, and so on.

In excavating the area, Watson and student volunteers discovered ruins of the stockade in which the workers had been kept. Everything in it had been torched. Eventually the team also found and "excavated seven graves," says Watson, "one of which was only a stain because the bones washed away."[52] Of the six sets of remains, five were of men, and one was of a woman. Since then, Watson and his crew have found two other sets of remains.

One skull they found had a mark indicating that the man had been brained with a heavy object and shot as well. Two other skulls also showed evidence of blunt-force trauma. Almost all the bodies showed signs of violence.

One man they only found when they excavated around a large poplar tree's roots in 2011 and 2012. The poplar tree—now just a stump—sits on one side of a hollow. At the top of the other side is a stone enclosure. Watson suspects it is a mass grave. Excavations resumed there in summer 2013. Studying remains from there will help tell how many of the laborers died from cholera and how many perished at the hands of a lynch mob, which the professor suspects was the case for many.

Watson told this writer that, given the deep anti-Catholic prejudice prevalent at the time, not only in southeast Pennsylvania but in the entire nation, "it is impossible to disentangle their treatment from their religion."[53] Indeed, he claims that there were women religious willing to come from Philadelphia to give the men medical care, but Duffy and others would not allow them access.

"Religion played into their death," asserts Dr. Watson, "no doubt about it."

CHAPTER FOURTEEN

Bl. André Grasset

+ WHAT I SAW AT THE FRENCH REVOLUTION +

In school most of us learned the French Revolution was good, that it was inspired by the one in America, and that it overthrew the big bad French monarchy led by King Louis XVI and his wife, Queen Marie Antoinette. Both lost their heads, Marie because she had famously said on learning the people were starving and needed bread, "Let them eat cake."

Except she didn't. And far from being "good," the Revolution was a horrifying, even evil experience. Indeed, historians call its first year the "Reign of Terror." It was characterized by hatred and murder, much of which the revolutionaries directed against Catholics. For in addition to overthrowing the monarchy, the Revolution also sought to abolish the Church and replace it with the atheistic Cult of Reason.

In 1790, the revolutionaries had begun their attempt to dismantle Catholicism by enacting the Civil Constitution on the Clergy. It required the people to elect both bishops and priests. Furthermore, if priests hoped to maintain their ministry, they had to take an oath of allegiance, not to the pope or bishop but to the state.

Only four bishops and about thirty thousand clergy—roughly a third of the priests nationwide—succumbed to governmental pressure to take the oath. Faced with so many "refractory" (noncompliant) priests, the legislature ordered their deportation in 1792. This marked the beginning of several years of intense and often gruesome persecution of faithful Catholics.

This brings us to our present subject, Bl. André Grasset. His family had emigrated from France to Québec in 1749, and they moved to Montreal in 1752. There Monsieur Grasset began his service as secretary to two governors. Six years later, on April 3, 1758, André came into the world.

Life was good in Canada until the "War of the Conquest," which Americans call the French and Indian War. The British victory in 1763 ended New France for good. Many French families, especially ones such as the Grassets who had served the colony's administration, returned to their native land.

Discerning a call to the priesthood, André received holy orders for the Archdiocese of Sens, where his archbishop made him treasurer and a canon of the cathedral not long before the Revolution began. When it came his turn to swear to the Civil Constitution of the Clergy, Grasset naturally refused. He went into hiding at the house of the Congregation of Jesus and Mary in Paris. Arrested here, he was taken to the Prison of the Carmelites, which the revolutionaries had created out of a former Carmelite monastery. There he and 190 other clergy—including three bishops—perished in the massacre of September 2, 1792, one of the Revolution's bloodiest days, which is really saying something.

What happened is that late one afternoon in the convent cloister, Commissioner Stanislas-Marie Maillard held a kangaroo court. As each religious or priest came into the courtyard, Maillard asked that man if he would sign the Civil Constitution of the Clergy. When the person refused, he was speared or bayonetted. The slaughter lasted throughout the night, and one witness recalled how he saw the bodies piled high.[54]

Many of the martyrs' bones were later placed in a glass shrine in the Carmelite prison, which is now the Catholic Institute of Paris.[55] On the site of the execution lies a marble slab that reads, *Hic ceciderunt* ("Here they perished").

Although one could say that Fr. Grasset was more French than Canadian, he certainly qualifies as Canadian by birth. Furthermore, those who buried him did so in the Canadian section of a Parisian cemetery. Pope Pius XI beatified him on October 11, 1926.

Why Bl. André Grasset Deserves Our Attention and Devotion

What are words, really? After all, Bl. André could have signed the silly oath and said in his heart and mind, "I'm not *really* agreeing to this." That would have kept him alive and left at least one more "sorta faithful" priest in the country.

Bl. André and the other martyrs understood that compromising or cooperating with evil would lead to scandal, even schism. If they took the oath, the authorities could point them out to other Christians and say, "See? They're priests. If it's OK for them to go along with the government's demands, what makes you so special? Sign or die."

In other words, their cooperation would have made the Church the slave of the state. They refused compromise, though, so that others would know how true Christians behave when faced with such a "choice."

We all face such tempting compromises, such as politicians who vote against the Culture of Life because if they don't, it will cost them their career, and "Look what good I am/could be doing in other areas."

We need Bl. André's conviction to stay strong in our faith and to hold fast to its demands.

God, from the beginning tyrants and governments have sought to compromise the Church by replacing her authority—which is really yours—with theirs. They try to make her and the faithful subordinate their consciences to the State, knowing that if either capitulates in one area, then other, even greater compromises will surely follow.

Help us, Lord, and those who lead us—our bishops—stand strong for your Church and her teachings. Help all leaders—secular and religious—work for the common good at all times. We ask this in your name, through Christ our Lord.

CHAPTER FIFTEEN

Fr. José Antonio Díaz de León, O.F.M.

+ TEXAS'S LAST PRIEST STANDING +

If you know from personal experience the meaning of the phrase, "No good deed goes unpunished," then you will identify with our next subject, Fr. José Antonio Díaz de León, O.F.M.

Born in Mexico in 1787, José entered the Franciscans at age twenty-four and transferred the next year to the College of Nuestra Señora de Guadalupe de Zacatecas. Four years later, he received ordination, and his superiors sent him first to Ciudad Victoria, Tamaulipas state, which borders the southeastern tip of Texas. The next year they sent him 380 miles north, to Mission Nuestra Señora del Refugio in today's Refugio, Texas. It's important to remember that Texas was under Mexican rule at this time.

Four years later, in 1820, Father received another assignment, this one to Mission San José y San Miguel de Aguayo, outside of San Antonio and the largest of that city's missions. Additionally, by 1822 he was ministering—by himself—to four other neighboring missions. And as if he didn't have enough on his plate, for a short while he also served as chaplain to the La Bahía presidio (near Goliad, Texas), ninety-two miles away.

In the early 1820s, large numbers of people were moving into the area, most of them from the American south and most of them Protestant. These settlers, a number of whom had enormous amounts of wealth, greatly coveted mission lands. The mission Indians stood in the way of their getting that real estate. As a consequence, they successfully lobbied for passage of a bill in the Mexican Congress that demanded those properties' secularization.

Thus in 1823, Fr. Díaz de León had to abandon the San Antonio missions. However, the Karankawa Indians needed him at his old mission in Refugio, which had fallen on hard financial times. Despite his best efforts to get them help, all he received was fifty pesos from Gov. José Félix Trespalacios.

Although ordered to transfer mission properties immediately, he began a series of delaying tactics. He deluged the Mexican bureaucracies with petitions on behalf of the indigenous population. Thus he kept the last two missions—Espíritu Santo and Refugio—alive for seven years.

In time, however, the government official who had given support to Refugio withdrew it. Fr. Díaz de León was left to try to at least save Espíritu Santo. He went before the government to argue that the mission's twelve Coahuiltecan Indian families had legal right to the district. Not surprisingly, the nearest town council objected.

In the meantime, the now-homeless indigenous from Refugio joined other Karankawa along the coast to harass the increasing number of white people moving into the area. The Mexican government then reestablished Refugio as the best way to ensure peace. Another priest was left in charge there.

Nuevo León's bishop had a vocations shortage and thus needed personnel. Therefore, he withdrew the priest at Refugio and authorized Fr. Díaz de León's superiors in Zacatecas to make him head of the last two missions. Father had a team of one, himself, so it was good that he was hardworking and conscientious. This situation lasted for three years.

With ever more settlers came ever more pressure to secularize the missions, that is, to give the land to the white newcomers and Mexican land agents. That, of course, would leave the Indians without property or a home. The settlers won. In part because of this, the Coahuiltecan Indians are now extinct.

After the secularization of mission lands, Fr. de León, while still a Franciscan, became an incardinated priest of the Nuevo León diocese, and the bishop made him pastor at Nacogdoches, Texas. Someone claiming to be a white Catholic land agent in the area wrote an anonymous letter to the diocesan chancery, saying that any Catholic presence in the area, even that of a parish priest, was dangerous because of the colonists' anti-Catholic sentiments. When informed of this, Fr. Díaz de León shrugged and moved to his new post anyway.

Upon arrival Father found soldiers using his church as a barracks, and they refused to leave. Father rented a house to serve as a chapel, but he couldn't make the rent. Not a quitter, he established a "piety board" to raise funds for a new church. While waiting for this effort to bear fruit, Padre threw himself into civic life, joining the health board, for instance.

Since Mexico was an officially Catholic state, all birth, baptismal, and wedding certificates had to be signed by a Catholic priest, and all marriages had to be conducted by a priest, regardless of the religion of the persons involved. This provided Father the opportunity to meet most of the people in town and in the surrounding district. Indeed, even if he had no official duties to conduct, he regularly rode around the region visiting everyone he came upon.

Because Father couldn't speak English well, many whites ignored him. Besides, many were only Catholic to the extent the law required them to be. However, given his sincere intent to befriend everyone, most people genuinely loved or at least liked him.

One interesting bit of trivia concerning Díaz de León is that in 1833, he baptized Texas pioneer Sam Houston. However, it seems that Houston was baptized mostly for legal reasons. Fourteen years later his wife convinced him to become a Baptist.

In any event, relations between Mexicans and white colonists grew ever more tense, exacerbated by the Mexican government's 1834 unjust arrest of Stephen F. Austin, the "Father of Texas." By this time the government had passed a law of religious toleration, which meant that Protestants no longer had to fake being Catholics. As a result, settlers became a little bit more open about their prejudice against Fr. Díaz de León. Someone even put out a contract on him, and he received death threats. Knowing somebody would carry out on those sooner rather than later, he wrote letters bidding people good-bye.

Sure enough, on November 4, 1834, as Father returned to Nacogdoches from a parish visitation, someone shot him near St. Augustine. He was not only the last Franciscan in Texas, he was the last priest in the state for several years.

An inquest into his death concluded he had become so distressed from knowing that someone would soon assassinate him, he committed suicide. Question: Why would someone who had served faithfully for thirty years, who had waged battle on behalf of the Indians against what we would today call the big-money interests, who had braved the often-violent Comanche, who had braved the threats that tried to keep him away from Nacogdoches, who valued holiness and knew what the Church taught about suicide—why would such a person all of a sudden become so unnerved at the threat of assassination as to kill himself? What? Did he think, "I'll kill myself before I give them the satisfaction?" Did he fear for his life so much that he took his life? His ministry shows a dedication and a hope for the future that suicides almost never have. Suicidal people are more apt to sleep the day away than venture long distances to feed souls with the sacraments. The suicide charge is patently ridiculous.

Padre Díaz de León would not be replaced by another priest until 1847. Meanwhile, Nacogdoches's Mexican Catholics fell prey to the prejudice of their white neighbors, who perpetrated the worst injustices on them. The least of these was burning the parish Father had labored so hard to build, which happened shortly after Father's death.

Why Fr. Díaz de León Deserves Our Attention and Devotion

Father shows us that while the faith calls us to be meek and humble, it also demands that we fight injustice in defense of the weak out of love for Christ. For seven years, this man made a lot of enemies because of his service to the native people. Then again, he knew he wasn't in a popularity contest. Rather he was, if you will, in a service or love contest.

Looking at our lives, can we say the same? If not, why not? What can we do to change?

Holy Spirit, through the example and prayers of Fr. Díaz de León, open our eyes to injustice so that we may confront it. Open our hearts that we may love and serve our neighbors. Cleanse us of any concern for popularity or vainglory, of any desire to be honored, especially if these stand in our way of making present the kingdom of God. In Christ's name we pray.

Early Twentieth Century

Early twentieth–century America saw a cooling down of the hot-blooded, red-meat prejudice that Catholics had previously faced. That is not to say, however, that Catholics had become universally accepted. In fact, they faced the same bigotry as Jews. Indeed, after the reestablishment of the Ku Klux Klan (KKK) around 1915, it opposed not only blacks but Jews and Catholics, too. Furthermore, it wasn't his lack of hair that cost Catholic Democrat Al Smith the 1928 presidential election.

The situation was a little better in Canada. The Church's full-throated opposition to the ill-fated rebellions of 1837–1838 had greatly increased her esteem in the eyes of the government, and thus her power and prestige. Over the next 120 years, for instance, the Church became the dominant institution in Québec.

That is, until that province's Liberal Party gained control in 1960. This led to the famous "Quiet Revolution," so-called because the new government so rapidly secularized society. To note just one effect of that period, the Québecois went from having the highest birthrate in Canada at the beginning of the decade to having the lowest by its end.

Our Sunday Visitor reported that between 1912 and 1928, there were 5,504 anti-Catholic propagandists at work in the United States and Canada, including 102 Klan officials; 133 "ex-priests," only forty-five of whom were ever ordained (the rest were frauds, although the true statuses of thirty-two were never discovered); six "ex-monks" (only one was confirmed to have taken vows; two were frauds; three were unknowns); and twenty-three "ex-nuns" (only five verified as real and thirteen confirmed as frauds).[56] In this same period North America saw the founding of anti-Catholic journals whose sole purpose was to defame and otherwise attack the Church.

To a certain extent this is all readily understandable. For starters, many North Americans still saw Catholicism as the ultimate bogeyman hiding under the bed, ready to pounce on good Protestants caught napping unawares. Indeed, considering such sincere and deep-seated convictions, anything less than Protestants' wide-awake, even hyper-vigilance would have been not only irresponsible but suicidal.

Furthermore, keep in mind that our holy faith has never renounced the goal that all who profess Christ will someday be united under his vicar on earth in the one, true religion that subsists in the Catholic Church. Throughout history this point has been driven home time and again (see *Catechism of the Catholic Church*, 2104–2109). It is not hard to understand why this still gives some of our separated brethren pause.

Nonetheless, only two of the martyrs described here spilled their blood on North American soil. Most died spreading the Gospel overseas. All offer great modern witness to the faith.

These are their stories.

CHAPTER SIXTEEN

Servant of God Leo Heinrichs, O.F.M.

+ He Died Giving Jesus to His Killer +

Born on the Feast of the Assumption, August 15, 1867, at Oestrich, Germany, near Cologne, Joseph Heinrichs felt a priestly vocation to the Franciscans from a very young age. However, just after he entered the minor seminary and received the name Leo, the Franciscans fled Germany to the United States to escape their government's persecution of the Church. This is how in 1886, Joseph entered the Franciscan Friary of St. Bonaventure in Paterson, New Jersey.

After his ordination in 1891, Fr. Heinrichs spent ten years at St. Bonaventure Church. He next held pastorates in Little Falls, New Jersey, and Croghan, New York, before assuming the same duty back at Paterson for three years. Then he took what would be his last assignment, as pastor at St. Elizabeth Church in Denver, Colorado.

Father was not originally scheduled to celebrate the 6:00 A.M. Mass that Sunday in February 1908 on which he died. He only did so because the slated friar was too ill to rise from bed.

Picture the scene. Nothing unusual happened during the liturgy until it came time for Communion. Now, from the time of the Church Fathers until the late twentieth century, people didn't receive Communion standing up as we do today. Instead, separating the sanctuary (the altar area) from the rest of the church was the altar rail. People would make their way toward this and then kneel along it. The next group would ready themselves behind them, and everyone else would wait in line down the aisle, just as we do now.

The celebrant would walk along the altar rail to distribute Communion, sometimes by himself, sometimes assisted by another priest. He would tell each person, *Corpus Dominus nostri Iesu Christi custodiat animam tuam in vitam aeternam. Amen.* (May the Body of our Lord Jesus Christ preserve your soul to life everlasting. Amen.). Then he would make the Sign of the Cross with the Host before placing it on the person's tongue. The communicant then would make the Sign of the Cross and return to the pew, and the next person would kneel down. (Interestingly, a small but growing number of parishes have reinstituted this practice.)

That Sunday, as Fr. Heinrichs made his way up and down the altar rail distributing Communion, a man sitting in the third pew on the pulpit side stood and got into line. No one in the parish recognized him. He knelt at the rail.

As *The New York Times* put it, "Father saw in the man about to take his life only one of the penitents to whom his heart had always gone out in love."

The *Times* goes on:

> The priest placed the sacrament on the man's tongue, and he pretended to take it. Then the assassin spat it out. As he did so, he quickly drew a revolver.
>
> "Look out, Father," screamed a little altar boy.
>
> Before the priest could move, the Italian placed the revolver almost against his communion robes directly over his heart and pulled the trigger. There was a muffled report.
>
> Father Leo fell in front of the altar. "My God, my God," he gasped and died.[57]

This man who had knelt as if to receive the Bread of Life had instead taken the life of a priest, who Catholic theology teaches stands *in persona Christi*, in the place of Christ. It was a horrible crime.

After the initial shock wore off, some of the male parishioners caught the assailant, an Italian atheist and anarchist named Giuseppe Alia. When later interrogated, Alia admitted, "I just went there because I have a grudge against all priests in general. They are all against the workingman.... I did not care whether he was a German priest.... They are all in the same class.... I shot him, and my only regret is that I could not shoot the whole bunch of priests in the church."[58]

Father had worked hard for the poor (the "workingman" Alia accused him of opposing) and was beloved by the parish children. He was exceptionally pious. Following his death the friars learned he had practiced many corporal mortifications. For instance, his bed was a wooden door. Although his usual practice was to go to confession every Tuesday, for some reason Father received the sacrament the night before his death.

Additionally, sources say he wished to die at the feet of the Blessed Virgin. An eyewitness saw Father breathe his last with a smile on his face, at the foot of the Lady altar to the left of the sanctuary.

The funeral Mass drew five thousand mourners, and when his body was returned to the provincial house (then in Paterson, New Jersey), some twenty thousand came to view his bier.

In 1912, the friars reburied him. Despite there being little left of his clothes or coffin, Father's body, especially the head and face, lay essentially incorrupt (that is, it had not decayed).

As for Alia, a jury convicted him on March 12, 1908. He swung from the gallows that July, unrepentant to the last.

Why Fr. Leo Heinrichs Deserves Our Attention and Devotion

After he fell, Father's last action was to pick up the Hosts that had spilled from the ciborium onto the floor. He did that so Our Lord's precious Body and Blood wouldn't be any more profaned than it had already been. To have this be his dying thought was truly heroic.

When we receive Communion, what are our thoughts? Are we distracted, looking around, thinking about other things? Or do we welcome Jesus into our bodies and souls?

Dominus Iesu Christi, help us realize the unique, humbling, and all-praiseworthy gift you have left us in the Eucharist—your Body, Blood, soul, and divinity. How blessed we are. The graces you give us through it are enough to make us saints with just one reception. How many venial sins you forgive through it—all of them! You are so good, loving, and merciful for humbling yourself by coming to us under the mere appearance of bread and wine. How easy it is to forget that what looks like these things made by human hands is actually you, Divine Mercy.

Lord, as we approach your altar to receive you, help us focus solely on you, as did your Servant Leo. Help us recall Mother Teresa's prayer, that if our hearts are for some unknown reason unworthy, you would give us the Immaculate Heart of your Blessed Mother with which to receive you.

We ask these things through you, the Father, Son, and the Holy Spirit, who live and reign, one God, forever and ever.

CHAPTER SEVENTEEN

Fr. James Coyle

+ FRONT PORCH MARTYR +

Many of us know about the insane bigotry that caused, say, the Nazi Holocaust and the Jim Crow laws in the southern United States. It's hard to imagine that kind of hatred toward Catholics. And yet, as we've already seen in this book, there have been times when wise Catholics on this continent kept their heads down and didn't draw attention to themselves. This, then, puts the story of the last known martyrdom on North American soil in context.

Born March 23, 1873, in Ireland, Fr. James Coyle was extremely bright. He received holy orders at the very young age of twenty-three. His first assignment was to Mobile, Alabama, where he served as a chaplain for mission parishes and then at a local boys' school.

In September 1904, Father's bishop named him pastor of St. Paul Church in Birmingham, Alabama, then the state's largest city and home to its burgeoning steel mills. This thriving industry attracted scads of European Catholics, and they needed a young, energetic priest to serve them.

Imagine the Birmingham KKK's reaction to the changes happening in their city. By 1906, 29 percent of Birmingham's population was Catholic, and 15 percent black Baptists, for a combined 44 percent of the population. White Methodists and Baptists totaled 21.5 percent. In 1905 Catholics were just 1.4 percent of Alabama's population; by 1916 the Catholic percentage stood at slightly above 5 percent.[59] Irreversible papist domination seemed imminent, and the Klan took occasionally violent countermeasures.

In the face of this, Fr. Coyle was not one to keep his head down. First, he publicly defended Catholicism's teachings against the same fundamentalist distortions we face today. Second, he refused to change his habits, even if those left him vulnerable to Klan violence. Whatever the Klan dished out, he was ready to take.

What the bigots did to his parishioners, though, was another matter. One parishioner was demoted from police chief to patrolman through KKK influence. Father had to employ security guards for the church. All of this broke his heart. His flock loved him because he truly guarded them as their pastor.

Thus we can imagine how the events of the early evening of August 11, 1921, must have affected Father's parishioners. The day had likely been hot: August, Alabama, and hot naturally go together, like cheese, grits, and catfish nuggets. The average high temperature is 100 (not counting the heat index), and it rarely slips below 87 degrees. Furthermore, this was at a time when air conditioning didn't exist.

Fr. Coyle ended every day by relaxing on his front porch swing, trying to keep out of a stuffy house and stay a little cool. And that is where a Methodist minister and Klansman named Edwin Stephenson confronted him.

A barber by trade, Stephenson made extra money by showing up at the courthouse to marry couples, earning him the nickname "the marrying parson." Perhaps this is how he found out what had happened with his daughter, Ruth. She was pretty, young, independent minded, and totally constricted by her parents' short leash. St. Paul Church, a block from her house, held an otherworldly beauty that seemed to dispel her world's gloom. She saw its congregants leaving Mass on Sundays, and they didn't look like the idolaters her parents said they were.

Not long after her eighteenth birthday, both out of conviction and rebellion, Ruth converted. Persecution from her parents followed, prompting her to run away twice. Each time the police compelled her to return. The second time her father bound her to her bedpost and whipped her with a leather belt. Mrs. Stephenson pushed a cloth in Ruth's mouth to stifle her only child's shrieks.

There was a man in Ruth's life, Pedro Guzman, a forty-two-year-old Puerto Rican who looked much younger. The two had met five years before, when Guzman had done some work at the Stephenson home. Guzman proposed shortly after first meeting Ruth and several times thereafter. In July 1921, after months of abuse, Ruth wrote him, accepting his proposal. On August 11, after obtaining the license at a satellite courthouse fifteen minutes away, they returned to Birmingham, where Fr. Coyle joined them in matrimony.

When Rev. Stephenson discovered his willful daughter had just two hours before married a *Catholic*, it was too much. He learned that it was Fr. Coyle who had officiated. This papist had converted his little girl (the two had been front porch friends since she was twelve), and now he had celebrated her marriage to "a colored." Unable to find his daughter or her groom, he vented his ire by bounding up the steps to the unsuspecting Irish cleric and shooting him in the head.

Stephenson turned himself in, saying he'd shot Coyle because he had officiated at his daughter's marriage to a Catholic. Two months later, and clearly guilty, Stephenson went to trial. The defense team, paid for by the Klan and led by future U.S. Supreme Court justice and fellow Klansman Hugo Black, pleaded temporary insanity because of years of Catholic "torment." And because Guzman was a dark-skinned Puerto

Rican, Black played upon the community's pervasive racism (even though Hispanics were officially considered white).

At the preliminary inquest, Ruth testified against her father, saying that he had often threatened to kill the priest. She also reported that he often said that "he 'wished the whole Catholic institution was in hell.'"[60]

Stephenson claimed self-defense. However, two witnesses had observed no prior argument or scuffling. Indeed, as the prosecutor noted, had Father had a hold of Stephenson's suspenders, as Stevenson claimed, the two would have stood so close together that powder burns would have been on the martyred priest. There were none, though. Nonetheless, the jury acquitted this man after just four hours of deliberation.

Two years later Ruth and Pedro divorced, and by 1934, both were dead.

Why Fr. James Coyle Deserves Our Attention and Devotion

Father was a Catholic pastor with a job to do and the Gospel to preach, and he did not let bigots stand in the way. And because he was fearless, a coward took his life.

Today the KKK is less of a threat, but other groups are no less vocal in telling Catholics to keep their noses down and their mouths shut. Fr. Coyle's peaceful bravery shows us how to respond.

Jesus Christ, you call us to have meek and humble hearts. You tell us to be wise as serpents and gentle as doves. Help us to bless and love our enemies while always standing up for truth and justice, so that all may know true peace.

CHAPTER EIGHTEEN

Servant of God Ángel Baráibar y Moreno

+ "You'll Die Because You're a Priest" +

As we have seen, Spain is the nation, the Catholic nation, that gave North America its first martyrs. Today that country is still Catholic, so much so that no other denomination comes close in numbers. Since the nineteenth century, however, secular forces have waged war against the Church.

We see this in the "culture of death" laws passed in the 1930s and whenever the socialists have ruled, even over the last ten years. During the last century and a half, we have also seen the persecution of great saints such as Antonio Maria Claret and even monarchs. Persecution by secular forces was most especially evident in the nation's Civil War, from 1936 to 1939.

The Spanish Civil War had its roots in the same sort of liberalization that saw a diminution and sometimes complete abolition of the Church's ability to influence public life throughout Europe in the late nineteenth and early twentieth centuries. Then, following World War I, Spain's political situation was so unstable, a military dictatorship stepped in to rule from 1923 to 1930. After the dictator fell and the king abdicated, a socialist- and communist-controlled government was popularly elected.

Rightists actively sought to retake power, and the next four or so years saw a seesaw electoral battle between the two sides. This period also witnessed successive attempts by the leftists to persecute and marginalize the Church. It became so bad that, in 1933, the same year radicals torched 160 religious buildings, Pope Pius XI issued the encyclical *Dilectissima Nobis* ("On Oppression of the Church in Spain").

The staunchly Catholic military leadership opposed the secularists' agenda. Thus, when the 1936 elections saw leftists once again take control of the government, the armed forces launched a failed coup attempt. Nonetheless they launched a war of attrition, to retake their nation from the so-called Republicans. Led by Generalissimo Francisco Franco, the "Nationalists" won successive victories, and by March 1939, the war had effectively ended.

The conflict cost roughly five hundred thousand civilians their lives, and both sides committed horrendous atrocities. Nationalists killed people for their political views. The Republicans killed individuals because of both politics and religion, for they saw believers as cumbersome speed bumps on the highway of Marxist revolution. The Reds' new order could not countenance such obstructions. As a result, nearly seven thousand clerics, religious, and bishops lost their lives because of their faith. So did roughly fifty-five thousand laypersons.[61]

Why should North Americans care about what happened in Spain some eight decades ago? First, the Spanish situation and our own have many parallels. For instance, just prior to the 1933 and 1936 elections in Spain, many averred that a Catholic was not a real Catholic if he or she voted for the Conservative Republicans (then Spain's version of the Democrats, the Labor Party, and the Parti Québécois). Don't we hear similar aspersions cast today?

Also, consider how quickly the Spanish Republican forces began changing society with their policy of radical secularization. Then look at Canada's recent erosion of religious liberty and U.S. efforts such as the HHS mandate and its violation of religious conscience. This period of Spain's history provides us with a sobering lesson, one we ignore at our peril.

Ultimately, however, this is a book about North American martyrs, and that brings us at long last to this chapter's subject, Fr. Ángel Baráibar. He was just one of many Spanish-speaking priests who were either born in Puerto Rico and went to Spain or were from Spain and, when hostilities erupted, returned home.

Father's family were Spanish émigrés to Puerto Rico when it was still a Spanish colony. Father, though, was born in 1891, after the island became a U.S. possession following the Spanish-American War. His father, a tenured professor at the Higher Normal School for Teachers, had married a colleague. Tragically, she died at age thirty-nine giving birth to Ángel. When he was baptized at five months of age, his aunt stood as his godmother. Seven years later she became his stepmother.

At some point the family returned to Spain, and Ángel entered seminary for the Archdiocese of Toledo, receiving holy orders on April 8, 1916. Toledo's cardinal archbishop made his new priest a parochial vicar at Santa Maria in the village of Illescas, as well as chaplain to the nearby convent of Franciscan sisters. Father's co-vicar was a good priest named Tomas Alonso.

For the next seventeen years, things were fine in Illescas. Then the so-called Red Terror broke out. As a result, "the simple act of going to church to fulfill one's religious duties was something heroic, and brainwashed youth constantly harassed priests and laymen."[62]

Republicans used parish records to identify, arrest, and imprison noted Catholics. The government suspended all acts of worship and put Illescas's pastor under permanent guard. No one could see or communicate with him.

It didn't take long for the pastor to understand what was coming, so he escaped to his hometown. His two vicars, though, whether out of duty or because of a less acute sense of the forthcoming danger, stayed in town. This is how a gang of Marxist militia from Madrid was able to so easily capture the two priests and six other well-known Catholics in the war's early days for the purposes of executing them.

Don Ángel tried to convince the militiamen he was just a simple office worker who was willing to make bricks in Illescas's brick factory, but he fooled no one. A militiaman removed the cap that covered his tonsure and then slapped him on the head, saying, "And what about this here?" The man made it very clear to Father: I am going to kill you, and it's because you're a priest. Thus, about a hundred yards outside of Illescas, at the stroke of midnight on August 11, 1936, the Republicans shot their victims.

Why Servant of God Ángel Baráibar Deserves Our Attention and Devotion

Fr. Baráibar reminds us of two things: First, modern efforts to marginalize and even persecute the Catholic Church shouldn't surprise us. They're part of what we sign up for when we accept Christ.

Second, not every martyr pines for martyrdom. Don Ángel pretended he was someone else, and his co-vicar, Don Tomás, cried. Once their fate became clear, however, they accepted it and spilled their blood for Christ.

God may not call us to do the same, but we have to understand that being true disciples of Jesus comes with some sort of cost. The return, however, is priceless.

Holy Spirit, the Lord promised suffering for those who follow him. No one likes suffering. If God the Father wills that we receive a cross, however, give us the strength and resolve to face it with love, joy, and confidence, for we know you will never desert us.

CHAPTER NINETEEN

Fr. Gerard A. Donovan, M.M.

+ It's Just Part of the Day's Work, Buddy +

At first glance, our current subject wouldn't seem to qualify as a martyr. He died not because he was a Christian or a priest. Rather, those who killed him feared he would cost them their necks. Yet in a way he is most definitely a martyr, for his presence in China as a missionary for Christ led to his death.

Born in McKeesport, Pennsylvania, on October 14, 1904, Gerard "Jerry" Donovan was the youngest of Mary and master mechanic William Donovan's seven children. Growing up he was puny and bore a strong resemblance to actor Mickey Rooney. By age thirteen, he knew he wanted to join Maryknoll, and in May 1917 the missioners accepted his application. They sent him to The Venard, the Society's college in Clarks Summit, Pennsylvania (now Baptist Bible College, where the glorious chapel has become the library).

As Gerard was the youngest and smallest of the freshman class, his fellow students frequently bullied him. Rather than trying to take revenge on his tormentors, he boxed and participated in athletics. When he wasn't playing sports or studying, he spent hours walking the fields, riding horses, exploring the woods, and reading books: tons and tons of books.

"The little midget" (as the language of the time allowed) also liked practical jokes. A cook was making applesauce on a camping trip, and

Jerry stood nearby. The man asked him for the sugar. Instead, Jerry knowingly handed him salt.

Mostly, though, Donovan was a serious, deeply spiritual youth who dedicated himself to excellence, becoming a saint, and toughness. For instance, on a 1927 camping excursion, he became very sick. When other campers grew alarmed, he replied, "It's just a part of the day's work, buddy."[63] That "part of the day's work" was a ruptured appendix.

Fr. Jerry was ordained in 1928, and his superiors immediately wanted him in China. Just before his departure, however, he became so ill he required hospitalization. He had peritonitis, inflammation of the abdominal wall, and came within a half hour of death.

Father spent the next few years in recuperation at The Vénard teaching Latin and math. By 1931, he had recovered, and his superiors sent him to Fushun, Manchuria, in northeastern China. The rain-soaked day he arrived, he joked, "I can't find any roses strewn in my path, but someone has been wonderfully generous with mud."[64]

Donovan's first pastoral assignment was Changchun. His parish was in a beautiful part of China but one teeming with outlaws. The faithful told Jerry not to leave the city, but like the young everywhere, he felt invincible, laughing at the very idea of brigands.

His parishioners had good cause for concern, though. The parish boundaries were immense. To reach his flock, he had to travel long distances through mostly unguarded, rural areas. Yet Jerry feared no evil. Contributing to his boldness may have been the well-known fact that the bandits' code forbade the kidnapping of priests. He told people not to worry.

After ten months, Father took over the Linjiang mission in the steep, cold Changbai Mountains on China's border with North Korea. Bandits were active in this area as well. In fact, banditry grew so bad that the local prefect ordered all missionaries to avoid unnecessary travel. Father wrote him, "You should have seen how happy my mule was when I showed him your telegram."[65]

In August 1937, after roughly four years in Linjiang, Donovan's superiors transferred him to Hebei and Fushun. Around this time Father revealed a very useful lesson he had learned:

> It is not necessarily the brilliant man who succeeds out here, any more than anywhere else in the world; it is the man who can *keep at it* in the face of every challenge, small and great, which God sends him.[66]

After dark on October 5, 1937, Father was in church, leading parishioners through the rosary's second sorrowful mystery, when a stranger walked in. The sacristan asked him what he required. Medicine, he answered. Come back tomorrow, said the old sacristan, shuffling off.

Instead of leaving, however, the man entered the sacristy, where seventeen-year-old seminarian Francis Liu was preparing the censer for Benediction. Assuming the man needed help, Fr. Donovan followed him. This fellow then pulled a revolver and forced the priest and youth out the back door. There four other bandits waited to spirit their captives into the mountains under night's blanket.

We know from Francis Liu, who was later released, that the outlaws— teenagers who either didn't know or didn't care about their profession's code concerning priests—initially treated the prisoners well. You might too if you expected to get $50,000 Chinese in ransom. For his part, Donovan never showed fear or fought back. He even joked with his captors.

In the meantime, the police and army combed a thirty-square-mile (seventy-eight-square-kilometer) area for the kidnapped men but never came close to them. Several false reports of Father's release came out until winter. After one supposed sighting in mid-December, all such reports ceased.

On the morning of February 11, 1938, Japanese troops found Fr. Donovan's emaciated, frozen body on a winding mountain trail. What likely happened was this:

A larger, more ruthless bandit gang either kidnapped or bought Father. Given his weak stomach, Donovan could not handle the outlaws' sorghum diet. With the dragnet tightening around them, finding him something edible proved too difficult. Father grew ever weaker.

Eventually the outlaws realized that they would see no ransom, so they decided to put him out of their misery. After knocking him unconscious, they strangled him. He probably died sometime in late January.

Fr. Donovan was thirty-three years old, the same age as Our Lord at his death.

Why Fr. Gerard Donovan Deserves Our Attention and Devotion

Fr. Donovan put service to others above his personal safety and happiness. If he hadn't, we wouldn't remember him. Because he served so nobly, however, we laud and reverence his memory.

Are we willing to set aside our preferences in order to serve others? Can we turn off the TV to converse with a loved one? Give up an expensive espresso in order to donate to the poor? Encourage a neighbor who is out of work? Fr. Donovan teaches us to find something to do that is of service and then to do it.

Lord, Fr. Donovan said he was happy "because I have tried to do what I was told and go where I was told."[67] *By sacrificing his will to yours, he did not lose his freedom. Rather, he gained it.*

Help us gain the same happiness, knowing that you always have our greatest good in mind. "For I know the plans I have for you, says the LORD, plans for good and not for evil, to give you a future and a hope" (Jeremiah 29:11).

CHAPTER TWENTY

Fr. Robert J. "Sandy" Cairns, M.M.

+ He Sleeps With the Fishes +

Sometimes we want so badly to do big things for God, but that first requires doing ordinary things in extraordinary ways out of love for him. In Luke 16:10–11, Jesus observes, "He who is faithful in a very little is faithful also in much." Our next subject was faithful in very little things, so that when it came time to do the biggest thing of all, he didn't hesitate.

Robert J. "Sandy" Cairns was born in Glasgow, Scotland, on August 12, 1884. His dad was a miner-turned-bankrupt-shopkeeper who needed to support his family. Thus the Cairns family, including eleven-month-old Sandy, joined the stream of Scots emigrating to the United States. They settled in Worcester, Massachusetts.

He attended St. John High School. To get a head start on earning money for Holy Cross College, where he hoped to study before entering the seminary, he left high school before the end of his junior year. Having done so without his father's permission, his dad's response was to insist that he enter the workforce permanently. Thus for the next six years, Sandy worked hard, saved, and took night and correspondence classes galore. All of this helped him buy a laundry company, which he ran successfully.

He was also civically active, had a great social life, and had a serious girlfriend, a Protestant lassie. They would have married, but she refused to raise their children Catholic. Their breakup left Sandy feeling greatly confused and empty. He believed his malaise came from serving himself, that he needed to serve something larger than himself, but what?

One evening, after yet another night class, he asked a friend what his future held. His pal replied he would go to Holy Cross and thereafter become a priest. Then he asked Sandy the question that changed his life: "How about you?"

Those three simple words hit Cairns like an avalanche. He instantly knew the answer: He would enter the priesthood. He finished high school and entered Holy Cross College, from which he graduated in 1914.

At first he planned on serving as a missionary in a California diocese. When his friend Patrick Byrne entered Maryknoll, however, the idea of serving in the Asian missions had the effect of a calling to Sandy. He too applied for and received admittance into Maryknoll, and four years later, received ordination. After two years of further study, in which he learned everything one might need to know in rural China, his superiors sent him to Jiangmen, not far from Guangzhou (Canton).

From the moment Fr. Cairns arrived, he threw himself into his work. We see his dedication in photos of him giving shots to young children or posing with students at one of the several schools he founded. In a letter home he confided that he didn't know how he'd pay salaries for six teachers, $2,614.83 each in today's dollars. He expressed faith God would provide, and he did.

Fr. Cairns also staffed the chapel at Shamian Island, Guangzhou. A story has survived of how he helped make midnight Mass there in 1939 especially memorable.

His *Kapellmeister*, Rodolfo Baptista, had suggested the choir use Perosi's *Missa Prima Pontificalis* for the evening's Mass setting. Father readily agreed to this great suggestion. There was just one problem, Baptista revealed: He had no male voices for the choir. Cairns told him to not worry.

Several days later, Father informed Rodolfo that his male voices would be the German and British vice consuls (recall that by this point, Germany and Britain were at war), a French banker, a Swedish diplomat, and a wealthy foreign businessman. Furthermore, the priest had procured the services of a local jazz pianist as organist. On Christmas Eve, as parishioners approached the church, they saw it awash in light, courtesy of the local city government, with whom Father had pulled some strings.[68]

Fr. Cairns's final mission, however, was on Shangchuan (that is, St. John) Island, best known as the place where St. Francis Xavier died while waiting to evangelize China. There Father totally renovated the crumbling Shrine of St. Francis Xavier, and his work still stands. One year, after 162 islanders had attended midnight Mass, Father gave them their first experience of a movie. He loved his flock, and there was nothing he wouldn't do for them.

In its 1946 obituary of Father, *The New York Times* said that his missionary work even required him to fight off pirates. Once, he stood up in a boat in his cassock and stared at the buccaneers, and their captain simply let him go. After another encounter he wrote, "During the excitement and shooting, I stayed on deck behind a sheet of iron and enjoyed the show." The *Times* also reported that he "did heroic work at Shamian Island Refugee Camp in the Chinese-Japanese conflict and wiped out a cholera epidemic on [Shangchuan]."[69] Indeed, during the outbreak, he traveled to each of Shangchuan's thirty-two villages.

By the time the Japanese attacked Pearl Harbor on December 7, 1941, they had already captured much of China and had controlled Guangzhou for three years. Father actually got along pretty well with the occupiers because he refused to let them intimidate him, and they respected his bravery. Now, however, with his country at war with Japan, he knew things would change.

Indeed, a friendly colonel visited Father on December 12 and warned him, "You flee, not die. Not flee, you die." After the officer left, Father prayed before the Blessed Sacrament for over an hour. He then composed a letter to another priest, writing, "It is my duty to stay at [Shangchuan] with the people and administer the Sacraments."[70]

Four days later Japanese soldiers returned and placed Father and catechist Ching Wan-Nam aboard a patrol boat. A short time later fishermen found Father's Panama hat floating in the sea. For years rumors swirled that this proved Father was still alive. After the war, however, a collaborator admitted that once the boat was out at sea, Father (and presumably Ching) was shoved into a pig basket and dumped overboard. The date of his death was December 16, 1941.

Why Fr. Sandy Cairns Deserves Our Attention and Devotion

Holiness is the total devotion to Christ, expressed primarily in giving ourselves entirely for love of him and in order to become one with him. By this definition Fr. Cairns qualifies as very holy.

Heavenly Father, we long to serve you in ways pleasing to you, our good God. Yet too often we serve ourselves, leaving unused countless opportunities for grace and thereby holiness. By Fr. Cairns's holy example and prayers, help us to increasingly serve only you.

Post-World War II

The post–World War II era saw thousands of martyrdoms throughout the world. It witnessed the complete obliteration of the burgeoning Church in communist North Korea. Other Marxist countries placed heavy restrictions on the faith. Islamic nations treated Christians as second-class citizens and Muslims killed them because of their beliefs.

The Enlightenment, a specifically anti-Catholic movement whose antecedents we find in the Protestant Revolt, came into full bloom and began bearing its bitter fruit, secular humanism and atheism. In turn these birthed both communism and *de facto* worship of reason and science. Secular humanists contend that Catholicism is the enemy of freedom, equality, and previously unknown "rights." Thus many in the postwar years have come to believe that being a faithful Catholic is antithetical to being a good citizen.

This mind-set has historically been most pronounced in communist countries, whose governments launched determined and unfortunately very effective efforts to eradicate the faith. Furthermore, communist nations continue to persecute the faithful. In China, if Catholics refuse membership in its state-sponsored "church," they could face various punishments. In North Korea, a nation where owning a Bible or a rosary is grounds for summary execution, there is not a single resident priest, nor are there likely any Catholics left.

The stories that follow exclusively concern those who lost their lives under communist repression. Each teaches a valuable lesson that is startlingly relevant to us today.

CHAPTER TWENTY-ONE

Fr. Albert (Alphonse) L'Heureux

+ THE TRAPPIST WHO COULDN'T BE TRAPPED +

What is it about Catholic Christianity that inspires such vicious and vehement hatred, even when its adherents do nothing other than serve their neighbors for love of Jesus? This phenomenon has occurred throughout Church history, of course. One of the most compelling modern examples of it comes from Yangjiaping, China, where thirty-three men suffered martyrdom at the Trappist monastery of Our Lady of Consolation.

One of their number was a Canadian priest. The only North American in the group, his presence allows us to relate at least some of this gripping tale.

Other than the details of his martyrdom, we know little about him. Born Albert L'Heureux on Saturday, October 13, 1894, in Québec, his initial vocation was to the Jesuits. However, he asked to join the Trappists in order to spend the rest of his days doing prayer and penance. Why he felt this was necessary or even desirable, we don't know. We also don't know how he received the religious name Alphonse or came to be at Yangjiaping, just eighty-five miles (135 kilometers) west of Beijing.

By 1947, the sixty-four-year-old Monastery of Our Lady of Consolation, a name St. John Bosco had suggested, was the oldest in China. It also was once the largest Trappist monastery in the world. Pius XI lauded it in his 1926 encyclical *Rerum Ecclesiae*. It was a huge success.

However, given the abbey's strategic location, and with the Chinese civil war raging, the Chinese People's Liberation Army (PLA) abandoned the policy of the Chinese Communist Party (CCP) to not molest religious institutions. In April 1947, the army riled the local population against the "oppressor" monks. Then on July 1, officials arrested two monks tending livestock outside the monastery.

Twenty-four hours later, soldiers arrived at the monastery with arrest warrants for two of the priests. The court charged them with crimes that allegedly happened during the Boxer Rebellion in 1900. Never mind that neither priest was alive at the time. The sentence: Confiscation of the abbey and its lands.

The people, whom the monks had always helped and sheltered, needed none to tell them twice of the court's verdict. Darkness had already fallen, and the monks were asleep. When the porter answered the loud banging at the door, the rabble flooded in and trampled and beat him. Then they took everything not bolted down.

The mob came back after morning Mass, this time with soldiers. They ransacked the library, looted the pantries, took everything in the refectory, and raided the chapel. The soldiers then arrested the monks, confining them to the chapter room. Abbot Michael advised his confrères that their deaths were imminent.

Over the next several weeks, the monks endured hunger, beatings, and several show trials. At the latter, whether they protested their innocence or remained silent, the Reds clubbed them. Afterward the judge had each monk put in manacles.

Spies reported that troops from the Chinese Nationalists, or Kuomintang (KMT), the CCP's opponent in the civil war, were rushing from Beijing to rescue the monks. Therefore the communist's commander Li Tui-Shih loaded the still-chained monks' backs with large packs of the soldiers' food and marched them up narrow mountain trails. Soldiers beat those who lagged. Billeted at a confiscated home, seventy-nine-year-old Brother Bruno Fu perished that night, August 15, 1947, the anniversary of his final vows. Shortly thereafter another two brothers died.

Ultimately Li moved the surviving monks sixty-five miles away. Since he didn't have enough handcuffs, he used piano wire. The men had left dressed for summer, but the forced march drew them up into still snow-covered mountains where they experienced frigid rain. Here a French priest passed after slipping and gashing his head on a rock in the dark.

Finally the prisoners arrived in Dengjiayu village and were placed in mostly ruined buildings. They had no heat and no water, and food was practically nonexistent.

The Chinese showed special contempt for Fr. L'Heureux. Why? Well the bald, bespectacled priest with the kind face was strong in every way and athletic. He was practical, blunt, and matter of fact, although he could be the consummate diplomat. He didn't often socialize, and he possessed a droll, subtle sense of humor.

Before his capture Fr. L'Heureux had visited the monastery chapel every day to contemplate the Stations of the Cross and go to confession. Now imprisoned, he drew upon the spiritual graces derived from these practices, not to mention his Jesuit education. During interrogations, he constantly bested the communists' arguments. Showing their strong intellectual acumen, they retorted with clubs, beating him so badly he couldn't move afterward.

During this period, Father contracted dysentery, with its practically never-ending diarrhea. Due to his beating-induced weakness, and with his hands always bound behind his back, he simply messed his pants.

The Reds wouldn't allow him another pair or allow anyone to care for him. His bound hands also forced him to eat from his bowl like a dog.

A guard finally took mercy on L'Heureux and removed the wires. His swollen wrists had grown over them, and the ripped scabs revealed the bones beneath.

On September 12, 1947, Fr. Alphonse began crying something the guard couldn't understand. He sent Fr. Sebastian Pian to see what Fr. Alphonse needed. When Father arrived, Fr. Alphonse could hardly speak. All he could do was make the Sign of the Cross with his hand. Sebastian understood and knelt next to this filth-covered, lice-infested man as he whispered his last confession. L'Heureux died the next day:

> When the young Chinese guard went to tell the other monks of Father Alphonsus's death, he was said to have stated: "That man died very peacefully. He looks like the other man on the 'ten-figure' frame (the Chinese character for ten is a cross) in the Yang Jia Ping chapel." Fr. Sebastian wrote: "We took him and laid him out on a stretcher. He did not look like a corpse at all, smiling as he was, with his hands crossed over his breast. Bending on one knee, we took up the stretcher and as we walked, we looked at his smiling face and we prayed for him."[71]

Why Fr. Alphonse L'Heureux Deserves Our Attention and Devotion
Father's last name means "the happy person," and that smile on his face proved the communists hadn't won, just as Our Lord's Resurrection proved death's defeat. His smile was that of a man in Christ's embrace. "You will be hated by all for my name's sake. But he who endures to the end will be saved" (Mark 13:13).

Holy Spirit, comfort and strengthen us when people revile our faith. Through Fr. Alphonse's and his companions' prayers, help us endure to the end.

CHAPTER TWENTY-TWO

Bl. Nykyta Budka

+ A FAILED BISHOP BUT A GREAT MARTYR +

It must be humiliating to receive a prominent position only to publicly fail. Many would shrink into the shadows, never to emerge again. It takes a special person to experience such a fall from grace and still keep working for the common good.

A good example of someone like this is Bl. Nykyta Budka. Born on June 7, 1877, in Ukraine, his parents were peasants, and he could only afford school by tutoring his classmates. He received holy orders for the Ukrainian rite in 1905.

Between 1880 and 1912, roughly 128,000 Ukrainians emigrated to Canada. Those who were Catholics had no priests of their rite to provide the sacraments and thus were in danger of losing their faith. Consequently, Pope St. Pius X erected a Ukrainian diocese for all of Canada in 1912 and made Fr. Budka, then a seminary rector, its first bishop.

When His Excellency arrived, most of the "churches" were just prairie shacks. He had only twenty-one priests. He traveled over every type of terrain, using every possible means, in every type of weather to reach his flock. While his residence was in Winnipeg, he rarely stayed there. Home was where the need was.

Eventually, though, more priests from Ukraine came, and enough homegrown vocations emerged that he needed to build a seminary.

Many parochial schools were also needed. Additionally, Bishop Budka initiated night schools for illiterate adults, instituted summer catechism classes, and personally performed various corporal and spiritual works of mercy.

It was a tough time for Ukrainian Catholics because many Latin rite bishops found the Eastern rites inferior and obsolete. They argued the Ukrainians should abandon their liturgical heritage for the Latin rite. Simultaneously, Budka had to protect his flock from Russian Orthodox and Protestant missionaries. Then there was the prejudice of the native-born population, who looked upon Ukrainians with suspicion and sometimes contempt. Some criticize Budka for being forceful, but he probably felt like a shepherd surrounded by wolves ready to devour his flock at every turn.

He lost friends because he had little use for those who didn't whole-heartedly support the Ukrainian Church and its clergy. He also made alliances with some questionable characters. The British didn't trust him because he seemed too nationalist. Ukrainians didn't trust him because they suspected he wasn't nationalist enough.

Now, no one could impugn the bishop's character or his piety. He possessed only the clothes on his back. For love of his people, he became a Canadian citizen. One could not find a bishop more loyal to the magisterium. And because of his efforts, there are now five Ukrainian Catholic dioceses in Canada, including one archeparchy.

These strengths, however, didn't make up for the fact that Budka lacked discretion, was a terrible administrator, a dreadfully boring homilist, and a poor judge of how best to use his priests. He was as authoritarian as a martinet, unrealistic, indecisive, and socially awkward in any company. For all the good he was doing, his incompetence undermined it all.

Over time the stress took a toll on his health. Indeed, he became so ill, he had to spend time at the Mayo Clinic.

The bishop left Canada for Ukraine in 1927 for recuperation. He was supposed to return when he got better. That didn't happen. To be sure, he did regain his health, but sending him back was not a viable option. However, looking at this still relatively young man, the Servant of God Archbishop Andrey Sheptytsky, O.S.B.M., of Lviv, patriarch of the Ukrainian Catholic Church, decided to make Budka his vicar general.

This was a time of great persecution for the various Catholic Churches within the Soviet Union. Pope Pius XII wrote two encyclicals on the matter, 1945's *Orientales Omnes Ecclesias* and 1952's *Orientales Ecclesias*. So the Soviets' arrest of the entire Ukrainian episcopate on April 11, 1945, came as no surprise. The bishops' crime? "High treason," for collaborating with the Nazis during the war.

This was a total lie. Anyone who studies the episcopate's denunciations of the Nazis and their other acts of bravery knows that. Their real "crime" was a refusal to embrace the Kremlin-controlled Russian Orthodox Church. Why was this important?

Catholicism was synonymous with Ukrainian nationalism. The Russians wanted that obliterated. By doing away with the Church, they would do away with the locus of patriotic pride.

The Reds also resented how openly Bishop Budka preached against them. They sentenced him to eight years, but he survived only four, dying September 28, 1949, at a gulag, driven insane by torture and worked past the point of exhaustion in the local coal mines.

Why Bishop Nykyta Budka Deserves Our Attention and Devotion
It is said God doesn't require success, he requires faithfulness. Bishop Budka always did what he thought God wanted him to do, regardless of the cost. It's what made him brave and led to his being a martyr.

And look at the results. In Canada the Ukrainian Catholic Church is still vital, and because of Budka's and others' examples, in Ukraine, it survived Soviet attempts to destroy it.

Lord, keep us faithful to you, and prevent our getting distracted by worldly standards of success if those prevent us from accomplishing your will.

CHAPTER TWENTY-THREE

Bishop Patrick J. Byrne, M.M.

+ A Hero Among Heroes +

The remarkable thing about our next subject is that at first glance, he was just a good, ordinary priest. Looking at his life, though, it becomes evident that his apparent normality was anything but. To every situation he faced, he tirelessly gave his all, and this is what made him a hero among heroes.

Patrick Byrne was born in Washington, DC, on October 26, 1888. His call to the priestly life came in a tragic way. He and his brother were in their boat on the Chesapeake Bay when a storm arose and upset their craft. His brother slipped off the overturned boat, and Patrick could only watch him drown. He realized then life is short, and he wanted to make his count for something.

Accordingly he entered the seminary, and after receiving holy orders on June 23, 1915, he joined the Maryknoll Missioners. Because of Father's zeal, good judgment, and character, his superiors made him seminary rector, then magazine editor, then vicar general, then treasurer, and in 1923, founder of its Korean mission.

In 1927, Fr. Byrne became the first prefect apostolic in Pyongyang,[72] and after great success in that position, he was transferred to Kyoto, Japan, in 1935. Then, in 1947, the Church made now-Monsignor Byrne apostolic visitor to Korea,[73] and in 1949, consecrated him bishop.

Far from reveling in his new position, Bishop Byrne somewhat resented it. He wrote a friend, stating that his energy was sapped and questioning why he had received this assignment at such an old age.

What was Bishop Byrne like? First, he was very funny. Also, though saddled with a weak body, he was tough. Spiritually, he had a childlike devotion to Our Lady and took special pains to say the Mass properly and reverently. He hated it when priests or religious gave a bad example.

Even as a bishop, he made his bed, mended his clothes, and cooked his meals. Later, as a prisoner, when the guards tried placing him in better quarters, he humbly refused. He believed man's ability to conquer the natural world and achieve success could blind him to the eternal success that comes from conquering temptation.

Not that sanctity came easy for the bishop. He always found missionary life a huge struggle.

On June 25, 1950, the Democratic People's Republic of Korea (DPRK) launched the Korean War and quickly took much of South Korea, including its capital, Seoul. Though Byrne and his secretary Fr. William Booth tried to hide, they were arrested by the communists on July 2, 1950.

The Reds placed them and a wide array of other prisoners—GIs, nuns, diplomats, and more—on a train to Pyongyang, the DPRK's capital. There they were locked in a commandeered school from June 19 to September 5. The insufficient rations weakened many of their immune systems. As a result the majority contracted dysentery, Bishop Byrne among them.

As the summer turned to fall, U.S. General Douglas MacArthur began pummeling the Korean People's Army (KPA) and pushing ever closer to Pyongyang. For this reason, the communist army loaded its 815 captives aboard a train and sent them north to Manpo, near the Chinese border. They arrived there on September 11 and stayed for six weeks, until American planes began bombing the city. That is when the

DPRK decided to move the prisoners to Chunggangŭp.

On October 31, 1950, the captives were handed over to a tyrant they nicknamed "the Tiger." As soon as he took command of the prisoners, he began the march—never mind that it was night. From the outset he made it clear that his guards would shoot all stragglers. He himself machine-gunned sixteen prisoners. Some eighty-nine people died for falling out of line, including a religious sister who was dumped into a deep ravine.

The march took nine days and covered roughly 155 miles (250 kilometers). That is equivalent to two-thirds of a marathon per day by people who were either extremely aged, suffering from various sicknesses, enduring profound malnourishment, or all of the above.

Then there was the cold. When the continuously uphill march began, the first snows had started to fall. One of Bishop Byrne's shoes had developed a hole that exposed his foot to the rocky road, so that it was cut and frozen at the same time. To deal with the suffering, His Excellency repeatedly recited his favorite prayer, the Our Father. At least he had shoes. Many did not.

In his worthwhile book *March Till They Die*, Fr. Phillp Crosble, S.S.C., remembers a kind guard once giving the group extra food. "Everyone agreed that Bishop Byrne must have [it]—and so he did," only to give it to others. In coming months they learned that "Byrne never claimed his fair share of anything, except of work; and of that he always claimed more than was his due."[74]

Trying to keep everyone's spirits up in a desperate situation, the bishop also became the troupe's cheerleader, despite his having a collapsed lung. Once, when a guard beat him, he smiled and complimented the befuddled man on his technique.

At one point along the route, the Catholic POWs asked His Grace to give them general absolution.[75] Since the KPA would have noticed this, the bishop decided to stand at the side of the road as the men passed by after a rest period and administer the sacrament to them. However, when it came time to move out, he could not stand, and someone had to help him to his feet.

When all finally arrived in Chunggangŭp, the North Koreans billeted many prisoners in an old school whose floors, walls, and ceilings were riddled with holes. Given its mountain location, with arctic winds constantly blowing down upon them, keeping warm proved impossible. By now Byrne had several illnesses that morphed into pneumonia. Many other people had it too. The Tiger made everyone exercise each morning, no matter the weather or the prisoner's condition. Predictably, His Excellency's health grew worse.

With American planes flying overhead, the Tiger moved everyone four miles north to Hach'ang-ni, where conditions were even poorer. One morning the medic caught Byrne lying down during the day, a sure sign of sickness. This man ordered him to the "hospital," an abandoned home whose floor had collapsed and whose "door" was a straw mat. There was never any intent that the patients get better. The KPA simply sent people there to die.

The building was so cold that frost as thick as cake icing coated the walls. Bishop Byrne received a straw mat to lie on and another with which to cover himself.

Even though he knew he would soon die, Bishop Byrne rejoiced. He told Bishop Thomas Quinlan, S.S.C., "Tom, don't be sad. I have always wanted to lay down my life for our faith, and the good Lord has given me this privilege."[76] His Excellency died the next day, November 25, 1950.

Why Bishop Patrick Byrne Deserves Our Attention and Devotion
There were many heroes on the 1950 Tiger Death March, but Bishop Byrne certainly ranked at the top of the list.

His Excellency could be a hero when it counted only because he had been heroically generous with God when no one was looking. Had he been a mediocre giver before the death march, he likely would have been mediocre on it. Instead, his total self-donation produced the fruits of fortitude and service, and more people survived than otherwise would have.

Are we mediocre or are we committed to excellence for Christ?

God, help us imitate Bishop Byrne's zeal, enthusiasm, and kindness for love of you. Help us be true heroes for the faith by practicing virtue every day, in ways big and small.

Here is a prayer from Bishop Byrne's own soul:
O my God, help me by Thy mercy before I die to regain all the graces that by my folly I have forfeited. Aid me to attain the perfection to which Thou would lead me, and repair for me also, I beseech Thee, the harm that I have done to the souls of others.[77]

CHAPTER TWENTY-FOUR

The Columban Missionaries

+ THE GREAT LEADER DIDN'T FIND THEM SO GREAT +

Throughout history, there was always just one Korea, even when Japan or China occupied it. After World War II, however, Korea became a mini-Europe, with the Soviets and Americans claiming as much land for their side as possible. Neither nation wanted another war, so the United States tasked two officers (including future Secretary of State Dean Rusk) with developing a plan for partitioning the nation. Knowing nothing of Korea and possessing only an old *National Geographic* map, they proposed splitting the peninsula at the thirty-eighth parallel, because that seemed to divide Korea in half. The Russians accepted this plan.

This likely qualifies as the dumbest decision either side made during the Cold War. It left the North with hardly any farmland, giving the nation yet another reason to attack the South. It placed the South's capital, Seoul, a mere forty-five-minute drive from the border, making the Republic of Korea (ROK, South Korea) exceedingly vulnerable. This closeness and vulnerability partly explains how the KPA so easily surprised the ROK and won so much territory in the early days of the Korean Conflict.

This gives some background for our next two martyrs' stories.

Although the Maryknollers are better known, the Columban Missioners had also established a formidable presence on the peninsula prior to the war. However, their superior and the apostolic administrator of Chuncheon, Bishop Thomas Quinlan, S.S.C., was captured along with Fr. Frank Canavan, S.S.C., and Fr. Philip Crosbie, S.S.C., in the war's early days. The bishop and Fr. Crosbie would survive the war, while Fr. Canavan would die in prison in December 1950.

Fifty miles to the east, an American Columban, Fr. Jim Maginn, S.S.C., was running the parish at Samcheok. Born on November 15, 1911, Father hailed from Ireland's "Fifth Province," Butte, Montana, where he lived the first ten years of his life. Then for some reason the family returned to Northern Ireland.

After graduating from secondary school, Jim entered the Columban seminary near Dublin. He received ordination in 1935, leaving for Korea the next year. Thus, by the time the Korean War broke out, Fr. Maginn had served the Korean people for fourteen years. It's not surprising, therefore, that he refused to heed his people's call to save himself by abandoning them.

The first KPA troops entered the region on the sultry evening of Tuesday, June 27, 1950. They did not reach Samcheok, however, until Sunday, July 2, not long after Fr. Maginn had celebrated his last Mass. On July 4, KPA troops arrested him. Like a lamb led to slaughter, he did not resist. In fact, he welcomed them when they arrived.

Before leaving with the soldiers, Father went before the church's high altar and said a last prayer before the Blessed Sacrament. When he emerged to let them take him into custody, the soldiers kicked and beat him. They were about to handcuff him when he told them that wasn't necessary, since he wasn't a flight risk. This left the soldiers speechless.

Father was pummeled, starved, and tortured. A jailer came for him one midnight. Father asked to say good-bye to catechist John Kim in the next cell. The troops granted this final request, and Father tousled Kim's hair before giving him his final blessing. "John, I hope to see you again in paradise," Father said. "Whatever the pain you have to suffer, bear it patiently, and never lose your faith in Our Lord Jesus Christ."[78]

The soldiers marched him barefoot up a mountain road, roughly two miles from his rectory, and shot him through the head, leaving him unburied in a ravine where he fell. A local Christian interred him, and in 1952, his remains were translated to Chuncheon Cathedral.

Another American was among the Columban Society's fallen. His name was Patrick Brennan. Born in Chicago on March 13, 1901, he graduated from Mundelein Seminary in 1928, received holy orders, and spent eight years as a parish priest. In 1936, following his heart's call to the mission field, he asked to join the Missionary Society of St. Columban. This permission was generously granted, and by 1937, Fr. Brennan found himself in Korea.

After the Japanese attacked Pearl Harbor, the Empire of the Sun, which occupied Korea, declared Father an "enemy alien." First he was placed in an internment camp. Then the Japanese sent him back to the States, where he joined the army. This took him to the European theater, where he saw action in Normandy, the Ardennes, and Germany. His actions earned him the Soldier's Medal, which is awarded for an act of bravery that took place outside of battle and only to those who put their lives at risk.

When V-E (Victory in Europe) Day came, Father hopped a troop transport ship for the Pacific, but the Japanese surrendered while he was en route.

Once demobilized, Father returned to the Far East. For a year he worked at his beloved Korean mission. In 1947, his order made him regional director for Asia, which necessitated a move to Shanghai. Then, just before Christmas 1948, the Vatican appointed him prefect apostolic of the Gwangju prefecture, with the title of monsignor. This was the same area he had served before, and the local church thrived under his leadership.

When war broke out, Monsignor and two other priests—Frs. Tom Cusack and Jack O'Brian—could have left with the other Europeans. The war left their people with such fear, however, how could they abandon them? Furthermore, what about the tens of thousands of refugees who daily poured into the area needing food and medical attention? The Columbans served all, and this resulted in not only saved lives but saved souls, even among the communists.

The three priests were at the far southwestern coastal city of Mokpo when the KPA arrested them on July 24, 1950. They and many other civilians were marched north to a prison in Daejeon, where all were crowded into a large, open dungeon. The last anyone saw of Monsignor was a glimpse of Cusack and O'Brian supporting his worn-down body.

Right around the time of the clerics' arrest, the South Koreans committed their own war atrocity. Needing to retreat, they had a problem: What to do with the three hundred thousand suspected communists they had imprisoned? Should they release them, fully knowing that many would join the KPA? No, they decided, they couldn't take that risk. The South Koreans killed everyone, women and children included.

In early fall DPRK officials found the mass graves. It is possible that what happened next was a reprisal for this war crime. Regardless of the reason, late in the evening of September 24, 1950, prison guards machine-gunned every last one of the twelve hundred inmates at Daejeon.

Why the Columban Martyrs Deserve Our Attention and Devotion

Fr. James Maginn and Msgr. Pat Brennan exemplify the Good Shepherd of the Gospels. "The good shepherd lays down his life for the sheep.... For this reason the Father loves me, because I lay down my life.... No one takes it from me, but I lay it down of my own accord" (John 10:11, 17–18).

Father God, thank you for shepherds who do not play the hireling but protect their flocks from the beasts seeking to prey on them (see 1 Peter 5:8). Through these martyrs' prayers, give us many more such shepherds.

CHAPTER TWENTY-FIVE

Servant of God Fr. Emil Kapaun

+ SO EFFECTIVE HE HAD TO DIE +

There is a reasonably old and venerable saying that an extraordinary man is extraordinary to other men but ordinary to God. One wonders, however, if even God finds extraordinary the Servant of God Fr. Emil Kapaun, a U.S. Army chaplain who died because, as his fellow POWs attest, his Chinese captors couldn't afford to let such a Christlike beacon of hope live anymore.

Born April 20, 1916, in Pilsen, Kansas, an ethnic Czech community, Emil grew up on his family's eighty-acre farm. On June 9, 1940, he received holy orders at what is now Newman University in Wichita. Father served as a diocesan priest before becoming an auxiliary chaplain in 1943 for the Army Air Corps at nearby Herington Air Base. That same year his bishop made him pastor of his home parish, St John Nepomucene.

In August of the next year, though, Fr. Emil entered the army's chaplain corps full-time, and from March 1945 to May 1946, he served in the India-Burma theater, where he earned promotion to captain. He demobilized in July 1946, and that fall, he entered Catholic University of America for graduate studies.

Afterward Fr. Emil returned to St. John's, but by September 1948 he had rejoined the chaplaincy. When his future fellow POW Bob Wood asked him why, Father joked, "Bob, have you ever had to deal with *an altar league*? I wanted to get back to a 90 percent male congregation!"[79]

While stationed at Yokohama in July 1950, Kapaun's battalion was ordered to Korea to counter the KPA's attack on the ROK. It was from this point that the Servant of God began showing the heroism that keeps loyalty to him burning in the hearts of his men to this day. In viewing YouTube videos and in speaking with these gentlemen about Father, one sees the welling eyes, perceives the barely audible catch in the voice, watches compassionately as these proud old soldiers struggle to maintain their composure in talking about someone they still love so much.

Not long after his arrival in Korea, a mine destroyed Father's jeep, so he used a bicycle to get to the fighting. When firing began, many fled from the bullets. Father would go toward them, since that's where he'd find the wounded and dying. On August 2, 1950, just a month after his arrival in Korea, such courage earned Kapaun the Bronze Star for heroism in action.

The battle that resulted in Captain Kapaun's capture took place around November 4, 1950. The People's Liberation Army (PLA) had joined the war because the DPRK was losing, and China didn't want an all-democratic Korea on its border. The PLA had cut off the main body of U.S. troops from their command post and medical station.

Due to Chaplain Kapaun's calm leadership, the command post troops and the wounded at the station did not panic. Instead they fought their way back to UN lines.[80] Capt. Kapaun, however, stayed behind. The army couldn't evacuate many of the wounded and dying, Chinese as well as American, and he needed to be with them.

The battle was really over before it began. Says Wood, "We were horribly deployed. We should have shot our regimental commander. Many of the troops were sick with pneumonia and dysentery. We were badly trained. Many of our weapons didn't work, and we were at half strength. The Chinese had a pretty easy time of it."[81]

Kapaun arranged for the remaining troops' surrender. Even though the Chinese promised to care for the wounded, gunshots coming from where such men lay soon belied that assurance.

Sgt. Herb Miller was incapacitated by his injury. A Chinese soldier had a rifle to Miller's head when he noticed a GI stomping across the road toward him. The unarmed soldier shoved the PLA trooper out of the way, picked up Miller, slung him across his shoulder, and made his way toward their imprisonment. It was Fr. Kapaun. Miller insisted he be put down. Kapaun responded that would mean the man's death. Miller stayed put.

The Chinese imprisoned the POWs at Pyoktong in the far north. None of the captives were prepared for the winter. The army hadn't given them proper clothing, only extra summer uniforms in which to layer themselves. Furthermore, the winter of 1950–1951 was one of the coldest on record in Korea.

Almost everyone had dysentery, and the barracks were small Korean peasant homes. Their captors sardined the men in so tightly that the only way to lie down was on one's side. The stench of all those unbathed men and the dysentery-fed fecal matter on their clothes was retch-inducing. Always, Wood says, there would be at least one delirious man in each room calling for his mother. It was a "horrible situation" and would have been worse if not for Kapaun.

Father went from bungalow to bungalow—even those of the enlisted men, which was against Chinese regulations—checking on the men. His leadership was such that every single night, at every single bungalow—of which there were dozens—he had all the POWs, no matter what their faith, saying the rosary.

Father fought for the captives as would the fiercest mother bear for her cubs, and he cared for them as a parent does for a sick infant. Even while he was sick, he would salvage tin from bombed-out buildings, take a rock, and beat the tin for hours into a watertight pan. Then he would put snow in the pan and melt it over a fire. He used this water to wash the sick and their soiled clothes.

Wood says, "He was a pretty good thief too. He'd steal medicine and food and share that with those who needed it." Many of the prisoners would live to a ripe old age because of such care. This writer has met some of them.

Father told the men to keep fighting to stay alive. "We're going to get out of this," Wood quotes him as saying. "These people are going to surrender before too long. We'll get through this."[82]

One inmate, Walt Mayo, had studied Latin at Boston University. Fr. Kapaun would tell him things such as *Ne illegitimi carborundum esse* ("Don't let the bastards get you down").[83]

"He was like a light of hope in a dark room," Wood says. "One man retained his civility, empathy, and kindness. Everyone else gave in to 'survival of the fittest,' and one man is showing them the way."[84]

Fellow POW Mike Dowe agrees: "He'd be talking to ['his boys'] and giving them courage so they'd actually want to live and be able to eat the cracked millet and cracked corn another day and put up with the whole situation."[85]

Father didn't walk on water. Dowe notes that the Chinese had a political officer named Comrade Sun who would routinely lecture Fr. Kapaun, which got on his nerves. Dowe recalls, "One day he was sitting looking out over the landscape, and I asked him, 'What are you doing, Father?' 'Well,' he said, 'I'm just looking down that road and thinking of the day those tanks will come over the hill, and I'm gonna kick that Comrade Sun's butt over the fence.'"[86]

Father would see the cruelty of their captors and say unkind things about the communists. But then he would immediately follow that up with, "Ah, Jesus wouldn't have done that."[87]

On Easter Sunday 1951, the Chinese specifically forbade Fr. Emil from celebrating the feast, "but like so many other things they told him, he didn't pay any attention to them," Dowe says. "He just carried on the service. The guards just stood and watched it."[88]

When Father contracted pneumonia, the Chinese ordered him taken to a place for the terminally ill, a building the POWs called "the Death House." No one ever came out of it alive. The thing is, Kapaun was getting better and, properly cared for, would have survived. However, Dowe says the Chinese "didn't know what to do with someone who had the sort of spirit he did. They just had to get rid of him."[89] They had to kill him, Wood says, because "he was the living embodiment of the teachings of Jesus Christ."[90]

By this point Father, racked with pneumonia and malaria, could not walk. This man who had done so much for others could now do nothing for himself. Four men, including Wood and Dowe, formed a stretcher out of a blanket. Wood remembers Father blessing the Chinese as the bier passed them, praying, "Father, forgive them; for they know not what they do" (Luke 23:34).[91]

Dowe evidently began to tear up, and the chaplain lovingly told him, "Mike, don't cry for me. I'm going to where I've wanted to be all my life. When I'm there, I will pray for all of you."[92] Two days later, on May 23, 1951, Fr. Emil Kapaun passed away.

Why Servant of God Fr. Emil Kapaun Deserves Our Attention and Devotion

On April 11, 2013, at the posthumous awarding of the Congressional Medal of Honor to Captain Kapaun, Father, it was said, was "an American soldier who didn't fire a gun but who wielded the mightiest weapon of all: The love for his brothers so pure that he was willing to die so that they might live." Father "reminds us of the good we can do each and every day regardless of the most difficult of circumstances."[93]

Dear Lord Jesus, through the prayers and example of your servant Emil, help us form ourselves ever more perfectly in your image. We ask this in your holy name.

CHAPTER TWENTY-SIX

Fr. Didace Arcand, O.F.M.

+ UNSUSPECTING, UNINTENDED, AND UNKNOWN MARTYR +

Many martyrs didn't know they would suffer martyrdom. They may have been captive and even slightly fearful, but their deaths came unexpectedly. Furthermore, their captors oftentimes had no intention of killing them, even if they wanted to. A good example of such a martyr is Fr. Didace Arcand, O.F.M.

Born in Champlain, Québec, on July 16, 1886, his parents named him Leon. Monsieur Arcand wanted his children well educated. Accordingly he sent Leon to St. Joseph Seminary in Trois-Rivières at age twelve. Even if he didn't have a religious vocation, his father figured Leon would receive excellent schooling. However, Leon grew increasingly convinced of his calling. He especially dreamed about converting Chinese pagans.

This isn't to say he never had doubts. During one summer break Leon produced a play and used the profits to buy a boat. He and his friends sailed the St. Lawrence River, and he fell in love with boating. It was such a powerful attraction that he questioned his vocation's validity.

He returned to school with his uncertainty unresolved. In the meantime, his favorite sister, Ada, age sixteen, died. Her father just made it to his daughter's deathbed in time to hear her say, "Tell Leon…"

That was all. The sentence went unfinished. However, upon learning her last words, Leon finished the thought for her. He had confided his doubts to Ada. He believed that with her last breath, she had told him to press on, so he did.

Leon spent much time at the Franciscan monastery next to the seminary. Since Franciscan life appealed to him, he applied for and received acceptance into the order around the summer of 1906. That fall he received his habit and the name Didace, French for "Diego." Initially, he didn't like the name, but when he learned that Ada had died on St. Diego's feast, November 13, he saw the name as providential.

The following fall he entered the seminary in Québec, where he took every opportunity to learn all about China and Catholicism's history there. After receiving ordination on July 25, 1911, God answered his prayers when his superiors sent him to Yantai, China.

China probably wasn't quite what he had expected. Coming from a land of law and order, he found the level of banditry and piracy shocking. Things didn't get better with time. In 1928, he wrote about being called to a dying man's side. Bullets whizzed by him as he exited his rectory. Didace recounted:

> I...sprang onto my bike.... I had scarcely gone a little ways when I found myself in front of a horse thief. He [simply] greeted me. Some ways later...I met three other brigands who ordered me to get off my bike.... I [ignored them and] continued my journey. There was a corpse in the way; it was probably a thief who had just been killed. Finally, I arrived at the patient's house. I quickly administered the sacrament and picked my way back home.[94]

After spending most of World War II in a Japanese concentration camp, Fr. Arcand returned home for a vacation in July 1946, just as the Chinese Civil War between the nationalists and the communists began. By Father's return in 1947, everyone knew the communists would win, and in October 1949, the People's Republic of China (PRC) was founded.

Initially the communists promised Catholics nothing would change. In fact, things changed rapidly. First, the government expelled foreign missionaries and religious en masse. Then it introduced the Three Autonomies movement, which later became the schismatic Chinese Patriotic Catholic Association. The Three Autonomies proposed that Chinese Catholics be (1) self-supporting, (2) self-propagating, and (3) self-governing (that is, no foreign assistance, no foreign missionaries, and no pope). The Chinese Community Party (CCP) wanted total control over all aspects of society.

Papal nuncio Archbishop Antonio Riberi and the country's bishops immediately comprehended the danger. To counter the government's offensive, they turned to the Legion of Mary. This is what got Fr. Arcand killed.

Let's back up a bit. What is the Legion of Mary, and why would it lead to someone's martyrdom?

Servant of God Frank Duff, an Irish layman, founded the Legion in 1921, and its purpose was to do good works, evangelize door-to-door, minister in prisons, and more. Although the Legion in China had its beginnings in 1937, it did not really take off until 1946, when it began to spread like wildfire in the face of the communist threat. By 1948, China had two thousand chapters. The Legion alone could match the Reds stroke for stroke. This is why the bishops used it to inform Catholics they couldn't join the Three Autonomies movement.

The government retaliated by expelling Archbishop Riberi and attacking the Legion in the press and on the streets. They also jailed Fr. Arcand and other chaplains. During his trial in August or September

1951, which resulted in a guilty verdict and a six-month sentence, officials forced Legionaries to read false accusations against Fr. Arcand. One woman refused. She disappeared.

Fr. Arcand's jailers never directly tortured him, but his health plummeted because of poor conditions. His cell was a wooden room equipped with a slatted door made of tree sticks. Many days the jailers didn't feed him until 4:30 P.M., when they distributed steamed corn-bread, some bitter herbs, bits of turnips, and hot water.

The Reds ran the manacled priest through the streets to let people see they did not fear to arrest even foreigners. The Reds wanted bystanders to jeer, but people stood silent as their faithful servant was humiliated in this way. Fr. Arcand took neither his arrest nor this little jog through the city seriously. He even joked with his guards.

Things soon became serious, however. Father was kept in handcuffs day and night, denied contact with other prisoners, and forbidden to speak or even move without permission. The Chinese also interrogated him while shining a huge flashlight in his face.

Around Christmas 1951 Fr. Arcand began suffering from urine retention, which left him screaming in pain. By early February he couldn't stand without help. On February 8, 1952, the Chinese finally realized the seriousness of the now-comatose Arcand's situation. Not wanting a martyr on their hands, they released him to a hospital, but it was too late. Father died that day.

A fellow priest who was still free claimed Arcand's remains. He noticed two small, unhealed wounds on the wrist bones, from the jailers' abusive use of handcuffs. Father Arcand's feet were swollen, which suggests that he had suffered for several days. Perhaps no one had noticed. In any case, no one had taken care of him.

Why Fr. Didace Arcand Deserves Our Attention and Devotion
Although Fr. Arcand endured harsh treatment at the hands of the Chinese, he expected ultimately to return home. Instead he became a sacrificial lamb. Reports say he never lost his smile. He lovingly accepted his lot as God's mysterious will.

When unexpected tragedy hits us, when plans go differently than we think they will or should, what is our reaction? Do we shake our fists at God, or do we remind ourselves that we are his and that he brings good from evil for those who love him (see Romans 8:28)?

God, through the example and prayers of Fr. Arcand, let us say as did Jesus when suffering overtakes and bewilders us, "Not what I will, but what you will" (Mark 14:36).

CHAPTER TWENTY-SEVEN

Servant of God Bishop Francis Ford, M.M.

+ A MAN OF MANY FIRSTS +

Our next victim shows that if you offer your services to God with a willing and loving heart, giving yourself totally and allowing yourself to be a pencil in his hand, he will do things with you that will astound.

Born in Brooklyn on January 11, 1892, Francis Xavier Ford was the son of a newspaper publisher and a freelance journalist. He experienced his call to the priesthood while in high school, and during his days at Cathedral College Minor Seminary in Queens, he decided to join Maryknoll. In 1912 he became the order's first seminarian.

Movie-star handsome and described as polite, cheerful, yet very quiet, Francis received ordination in 1917 and sailed for China in early 1918, with three other priests. When he stepped off the boat at Guangdong, Fr. Ford prayed that Jesus would make their efforts fruitful, even if that meant martyrdom: "At least we...shall become the King's Highway in pathless China."[95]

Father's work as a missionary stood out so much that, in 1925, the Vatican made him prefect apostolic for Méizhōu. Then, when that territory was raised to a vicariate apostolic in 1935, he became its vicar and was thus accorded the title of bishop.

Bishop Ford centered his efforts on creating a larger local clergy and religious and getting laity involved in a variety of apostolates. He also did something unusual for the times: He encouraged religious sisters to evangelize. As a result, women played a much more prominent role in the Méizhōu vicariate than was the case in many other places. Under Bishop Ford's leadership, his diocese's Catholic population grew to twenty thousand, up from nine thousand when he started.

When World War II broke out, Bishop Ford took an active role in the efforts against the Japanese, aiding downed Allied airmen and Chinese guerillas and assisting hundreds of refugees. Immediately following the war's end, the Vatican made the vicariate a full-fledged see. After the CCP triumphed over the KMT in the civil war, however, the Reds placed Bishop Ford under house arrest for espionage, as they considered all bishops spies for the "imperialist" Vatican.

He never received a trial, but this didn't stop the Reds from punishing him. They took him on a humiliation tour of the various cities that had enjoyed his ministry for nearly three decades. In each place, they paraded him along his own *Via Dolorosa*. The people he had served cursed, mocked, taunted, and beat him with stones, ropes, and sticks.

On these excursions the bishop could never defend himself because the Reds tied his hands behind his back. Once the people's torment of His Excellency was so ferocious that it frightened away his guards. The bishop, however, kept walking along the designated route.

When a wet rope dries, it shrivels. So in another place, the Chinese crafted a wet noose and placed this tightly around His Lordship's neck. That almost strangled him. They also forced him to get naked in front of his secretary, Sr. Joan Marie Ryan, M.M., and compelled her to look.

Finally the communists interned the bishop in a Guangzhou prison, where they ritually tortured him. In addition, they fed him so little that at his death on February 21, 1952, he was emaciated. Ryan saw another prisoner carry his emaciated body like a sack of potatoes. His black hair was a transfigured white.

Why Servant of God Bishop Francis Ford Deserves Our Attention and Devotion

Bishop Ford was first in so many ways. He was Maryknoll's first seminarian and in its first group of China missionaries; he was Maryknoll's first territorial bishop, the first to set up a Maryknoll seminary in China, and the first to establish a Maryknoll convent for women religious. He was the first from his order and the first American Catholic bishop to die at the CCP's hands. He accomplished so much because he gave himself completely to the Chinese people, who served as a surrogate for Christ.

Good and gracious God, the persecution suffered by Bishop Ford continues to this day. We pray for the emancipation of Chinese Catholics. Would not these brave souls who maintain their loyalty to Holy Mother Church receive immense comfort and fortitude by your servant Francis's beatification? You know better than we do, Lord, so we pray that your ineffable will be done.

CHAPTER TWENTY-EIGHT

Bl. Vasel Velychkovsky C.SS.R.

+ LOUSY COMMIES, I LAUGH AT YOUR PERSECUTION +

The Gospels describe two occasions when huge waves tossed the apostles' boats, and each incident greatly frightened them. Had Bl. Vasel
Velychkovsky been present, he probably would have said, "Eh, it's just
a little wind and rain." Nothing shook this man.

Born in Ukraine, he had many Eastern rite Catholic priests in his
family tree. (Married men can receive ordination to the priesthood in
many of the Catholic Church's twenty-two Eastern rites, although they
cannot become bishops.) Both his parents were catechists. They home-
schooled and raised their brood to serve Christ by serving others. All of
this gave Vasel a desire for the priesthood at a young age. Additionally,
he dedicated himself to the Blessed Virgin at the age of eight, which he
counted as the most important thing he ever did.

At fifteen, he became a soldier in World War I. When he returned
from the war at age twenty, he entered the Ukrainian rite seminary at
Lviv. He was ordained a deacon in 1924, and it was shortly after this
that he discerned a call time to monastic life. As a result, he took vows
as a Redemptorist the next year and received holy orders just a few
months later.

For the next two years, Fr. Vasel taught high school, where his gift
for evangelization became evident. For this reason, he started doing
missionary work among the region's Ukrainians starting in 1928. For
several reasons, many had become Orthodox. His efforts in bringing

Catholics home proved fruitful enough that he had to oversee the building of a number of churches and chapels.

Then in 1935 his superiors made him prior of the Redemptorist monastery at Ivano-Frankivsk. His main function, however, was preaching parish missions. He would spend up to two weeks in one church and face packed houses of congregants each night.

This was a period of great persecution for Ukrainian Catholics. The Soviet Union saw them as a potential threat because of their ties to the Vatican and because they weren't as easily controlled as the Russian Orthodox. The Orthodox saw them as heretics and traitors whose Church had no business existing. So with the NKVD (the secret police, which became the notorious KGB) and Russian Orthodox working in concert, life was uncomfortable for the Ukrainian faithful.

Still, find pictures of Bl. Vasel online. Does he look like someone to be easily intimidated? Not so much. In 1940, he led twenty thousand plus people through his city's streets, each of them carrying a cross. Now, he *had* to know the Soviets wouldn't ignore this.

They didn't. The NKVD arrested him. However, when the faithful seemed ready to storm the prison to rescue him, the police released Father. The Reds told him to stop his activities if he knew what was good for him. Father knew what was good for him: Jesus. So he kept going.

During World War II, his archbishop sent Fr. Velychkovsky to work in Nazi-occupied Poland. The Nazis, however, accused him of being not a missionary but a resistance leader. He fled and spent the rest of the war in Ternopil, in western Ukraine, ministering to the bombed-out city's sick, wounded, and dying.

After Germany's defeat, Fr. Velychkovsky hid in plain sight from the Reds, going throughout the countryside and giving missions. By spring 1945, however, the NKVD had arrested all of the Ukrainian Church's hierarchs. Summer brought the arrest of superiors such as Fr. Velychkovsky, who was incarcerated for speaking against communism.

In his interrogation, the NKVD officer told Father he could easily gain his freedom. Just join the Russian Orthodox Church, he advised. (Doesn't it seem odd that a regime officially and implacably committed to atheism was so eager to get people out of one Church and into another?) Bl. Vasel said no. Even if it cost his life, he would remain Catholic.

For two years thereafter the police tortured Father. Finally, a Soviet court sentenced him to death for things he had written in a 1939 pocket calendar, which no one else had likely ever seen.

Fr. Velychkovsky spent the next three months evangelizing and catechizing the other condemned men. Thus, many went to a far better reward than they might have.

One night, guards came to the priest's cell. He knew the drill. They would take him downstairs and put a bullet through the back of his head. But when they should have zigged, they zagged, upstairs. For some reason, the authorities had commuted his sentence to a ten-year term, and they sent him to work in some mines north of the Arctic Circle.

Each night after returning to his barracks from the mines, he would collapse from exhaustion. Nonetheless, he still somehow found the time and energy to make chalices and other liturgical items from discarded cans and celebrated Mass almost every day.

Near his term's end he was at death's door, so poor had been his treatment, so exhausting had been his work. Friends arranged his transfer to the prison hospital, which likely saved him. He left prison in 1955.

Father Velychkovsky returned to Lviv, where the persecution of the Ukrainian Church had so intensified hardly anyone would come near him. What was a little thing like that, however, to Velychkovsky? Renting a one-room flat, he used cardboard boxes to make an altar and celebrated the heavenly mysteries daily for groups of five or so persons at a time. The authorities knew he did this, he knew they knew it, and he didn't care.

The Holy See named him a bishop for his bravery. However, because of the Church's difficulties, he didn't receive consecration until 1963. Bishop Velychkovsky couldn't minister to people in any official capacity, so he turned his tiny apartment into a combination cathedral/seminary/chancery. He also wrote a book on Our Lady of Perpetual Help. That book surely gladdened the Soviets' hearts. He argued, for example, that atheists make bad citizens and Christians good ones.

In fact, the Soviets were glad enough about this and his illegal teaching of theology to give him a three-year prison term in January 1969. This time chemical, physical, and mental torture shaded every moment of his sentence. Consequently he contracted heart disease. So close was he to death, the Russians released him early. They didn't want a martyr on their hands.

After his release the bishop went to Rome. There he met Canadian Archbishop Maksym Hermaniuk, who invited him to live in Winnipeg, Manitoba. It was there that the effects of thirteen years in Soviet prisons took their toll. He died on June 30, 1973.

The bishop's beatification cause proceeded very quickly. Started in 2000, it ended with John Paul II's beatification of him in 2001. In 2002, when Church officials exhumed the bishop's body as part of the canonization process, he was found to be completely incorrupt.

Why Bl. Vasel Velychkovsky Deserves Our Attention and Devotion

Bl. Vasel's fear of God made him fearless. He lived in service to Christ, placing his life at Christ's disposal. Thus, whenever God wanted him, he could take him. Whatever hardships Velychkovsky experienced, he knew God's grace was sufficient.

Each Christian needs that same unshakable confidence if they're to fulfill Providence's plans for their lives. We won't necessarily endure Bl. Vasel's inconceivable suffering, but trials will come. We all need to expect them and prepare accordingly.

Lord, help us adopt Bl. Vasel's faith, confidence, and fearlessness. Through his example, let no earthly concern ever inhibit our service of you. Through his prayers and those of Our Lady of Perpetual Help, lead us to life everlasting with you.

CHAPTER TWENTY-NINE

The Other North American Martyrs

+ ¡*Arriba!* ¡*Arriba!* Up to Heaven! +

When most of us think of the countries that constitute North America, we typically begin and end with the United States and Canada.

The continent, however, is much vaster than this. It "starts," if you will, at Greenland and ends at Panama. It even includes the Caribbean islands.

Furthermore, many of the other countries within this vast continent have seen more than their share of those who spilled their blood for Christ. Sadly, there is not enough room in this present work to do justice to these other North American martyrs. Indeed, their stories would take up an entire extra book.

With that understood, let's not let the perfect be the enemy of the good, eh? Let's take a look, however brief, at the men and women who earned the palm of martyrdom south of the Rio Grande (Greenland and the Caribbean have no martyrs that we know of).

The first to lose their lives for the faith on North American soil were three boys. Their names were Cristóbal, Antonio, and Juan, and they were indigenous boys who became Christians not long after Hernán Cortés conquered Mexico. Both Cristóbal and Antonio were sons of *caciques* (chiefs), whereas Juan was Antonio's servant. All three received Christ while studying at the Franciscan school in Tlaxcala. Cristóbal's father murdered him in 1527 when the thirteen-year-old would not stop preaching about the need to turn away from pagan idolatry and embrace the one, true faith. Juan and Antonio perished in 1529 at Cuauhtinchán, Puebla, en route to a missionary trip to Oaxaca. Both were also thirteen at the time of their deaths.

There were several other martyrs during the Spanish colonial period, including Mexico's first saint, St. Felipe de Jesús. Interestingly, he did not give his life for Christ in Mexico, but in Japan, where he was one of the Twenty-Six Martyrs of Nagasaki (possibly better known as St. Paul Miki and Companions, whose feast is February 5). Today, he is the patron saint of Mexico City.

Fast-forward to the nineteenth century: Under the leadership of a Catholic priest, Mexico gained its independence from Spain in 1821. At first, the government favored Catholicism and declared it the land's official religion. However, in the ensuing decades, power shifted into the hands of Freemasons, who exhibited all of that secret order's hatred of the faith. Ever so gradually, the government began confiscating Church property, closing down convents and monasteries, and abolishing religious orders.

Consider one of Mexico's great dishes, chicken mole, which was invented by nuns at a convent in the enchanting colonial city of Puebla. One can still visit the very kitchen where the sisters created the dish and look up at the wonderful frescos and other art upon which they would have gazed as they concocted this great culinary gift. However, one will not see a nun anywhere in sight, for this once magnificent convent is now merely a museum.

Exacerbating the Church's ever-more tenuous status was the fact that she threw her weight behind those politicians who supported her yet never retained power long enough to stem the surging tide of persecution.

Then came the constitution of 1917, which, as was noted in *39 New Saints You Should Know*, "made it illegal for priests to administer the sacraments or do any pastoral work such as holding retreats, making sick calls, or conducting processions. To make matters worse, a 1926 law fined them 500 pesos (today worth $2,900) for wearing clerical garb in public. Some local governors cleared priests out of entire states."[96] It also led to "the harassment and even murder of faithful Catholics. It is said the people would wake in the morning, go out to their fields, and find the corpses of those whom the *federales* had executed in the night."[97]

In reaction, the Mexican people launched the Cristero revolt (1926–1929), a civil war depicted in the worthy 2012 film *For Greater Glory*.[98] Amongst the people who lost their lives in this conflict were Bl. Miguel Pro and Bl. José Luis Sánchez del Río, both featured in the aforementioned book. Some thirty thousand other Catholics perished as well.

One of these was Mateo Elías Nieves y Castillo (also called Elías del Socorro), O.S.A. From its beginning, his life was filled with suffering, as if the Lord had a special need for him to share in the work of redemption that reverberates throughout the centuries. He almost lost his life at birth. As a little child, he was rendered blind for a time and also had to endure tuberculosis. His father was murdered when Elías was twelve, and the boy's mother passed away not long thereafter.

In some people, this would have provoked a "Why me, Lord?" or even a hatred of God, along the lines of, "If God really existed and really loved *me*, he wouldn't let all these bad things happen." Not Elías. The response it evoked in him was love, and through this generosity of heart, Jesus called him to the priesthood.

As an orphan, though, he lacked the resources to enter the seminary. Rather than let this stand in his way, he did what he could, namely

making himself a more perfect and virtuous Christian and fully partici-
pating in the life of his parish.

Finally, at age twenty-one, he was able to enter the Augustinian
high school (yes, high school, as a freshman). Elías made his first vows
seven years later, and five years after that in 1916 at age thirty-two, he
received ordination.

See? With God all things are possible. Did this saintly man experience doubts that Providence would not sustain him? Did he have
soul-rending moments when he reconsidered whether he truly had a
vocation after experiencing all of these trials?

We don't know. Even if he did, though, at some point he redoubled
his faith in God's calling him to the priesthood and trusted that Our
Lord would remove any obstacles that stood in the way.

In 1921, his bishop appointed him parochial vicar for the poor village
of Cañada, Guanajato state. When the great persecution against the
Church erupted in 1926, rather than obeying the government's order
that he remove himself to the nearest large city, he built a small altar
in a local cave and worked from there as an underground priest for
fourteen months. People attended Mass in shifts, a situation that only
stopped when Fr. Nieves determined this placed everyone in danger.

Around mid-morning on March 9, 1928, Father heard the stamping
of the horses of a platoon of soldiers. Rather than run, he sat on a
ranch's fence as if he was simply a farmer taking a break. However,
ranchers normally didn't wear glasses. Furthermore, the soldiers saw
the priest's black clerics peeking from under his outer clothing.

The major who commanded the troop asked Elías if he was the local
curate, and Nieves did not deny this. They arrested him and marched
him toward the nearby city of Cortazar. On March 10, 1928, just
outside of that town at a place called El Llano, the soldiers backed him

up against some mesquite bushes, where he asked for a moment to pray. He then blessed his executioners, gave them what little he possessed, stretched out his arms so that his body resembled that of Christ on the cross, and informed the captain in charge of the firing squad he was ready.

The captain mocked him, saying, "Let's see if dying is anything like saying Mass."

"You are speaking the truth," Padre Nieves responded. "To die for our religion is a pleasing sacrifice to God."

Disgusted at this, the captain shot the martyr, who was heard to say as he collapsed, "God forgive you, my son. ¡*Viva Cristo Rey!* ¡*Viva Cristo Rey!*" (Long live Christ the King!)[99] Then the captain administered the *coup de grâce*.

During the investigation into his beatification cause, no testimony was as impressive as that given by this same captain, Mañuel Márquez Cervantes, who said, "Fr. Nieves died a hero and a saint."[100]

Even after the war, the Mexican faithful lost their lives due to anti-Catholic violence. Amongst these was the movie-star-beautiful María de la Luz Camacho González, a Servant of God and laywoman. She died at age twenty-seven in 1934, when she was shot during a demonstration against Catholicism outside her church.

We should mention several martyrdoms elsewhere in the southern part of North America. For instance, there is Luis Boltel, a layman and a Cuban whom the Castro regime martyred in 1972. One particularly poignant martyrdom was that of Servant of God Archbishop Oscar Romero of El Salvador. In 1980, during his nation's civil war, he was shot through the heart as he celebrated Mass. Although no one was ever arrested for his murder, most experts believe rightist forces orchestrated it, even though he had not taken a side in the conflict.

There were several other casualties of the civil wars that infested Central America in the 1980s, including a U.S. priest from Oklahoma, Servant of God Fr. Stanley Rother, and four female missionaries: Maryknoll Sisters Maura Clarke and Ita Ford (first cousin of Servant of God Bishop Francis Ford), laywoman Jean Donovan, and Sr. Dorothy Kazel, O.S.U. In April 1998, Bishop Juan José Gerardi was assassinated because he spoke out against the atrocities committed by both sides during Guatemala's recently concluded civil war.

Why the Hispanic North American Martyrs Deserve Our Attention and Devotion

There have been many martyrs created south of the Rio Grande, and the Church has declared a good number of these blesseds or saints. Though separated by culture and language, we in the Anglo part of North America share a common bond in the faith with these Hispanic brothers and sisters. Particularly given the tensions that fray relations between the United States and many Latin countries, recalling this common bond ideally should serve to help us work past that which divides us. The martyrs overcame bigger obstacles than disputes about trade, borders, migration, drugs, and all the rest. If they can do it, so can we.

Holy Spirit, through St. Paul, you told us that in Christ Jesus, there is no longer slave or free, man or woman, Jew or Greek—or, for that matter, Canadian, Guatemalan, American, Mexican, Panamanian, or Haitian— for through our baptism, we are all one (see Galatians 3:28). Through the example and prayers of these martyrs and all the saints of North America, help us labor together in a spirit of Christian humility so that we may present the joy of Catholicism and the quenching waters of Christ to a world desperately thirsting for both.

Calendar of the North American Martyrs, with Place and Year of Death

Where the date of death is unknown, I assigned an approximate date.

January 23	Fr. Alonso Gil de Avila, O.F.M.	New Mexico, ca. 1672
c. January 25	Fr. Manuel de Mendoza, O.F.M.	Florida, 1704
c. January 25	Fr. Domingo Criado, O.F.M.	Florida, 1704
c. January 25	Fr. Tiburcio de Osorio, O.F.M	Florida, 1704
c. January 25	Fr. Augustino Ponze de Leon, O.F.M.	Florida, 1704
January 25	Br. Marcos Delgado, O.F.M.	Florida, 1704
c. January 25	Fr. Luis Sánchez, O.F.M.	Florida, 1696
January 26	Fr. Juan de Parga y Arralyo, O.F.M.	Florida, 1704[101]
January 27	Fr. Manuel Beltran, O.F.M.	New Mexico, 1689
c. January 30	Fr. Anne de Noüe, S.J.	Québec, 1646
c. January 30	Fr. Gerard Donovan	China, 1938
January 31	Fr. Ángel Miranda, O.F.M.	Florida, 1704
January 31	Lt. Juan Ruiz Mejia	Florida, 1704
January 31	Antonio Enija (Eniza), Indian	Florida, 1704
January 31	Amador Cuipa Feliciano, Indian	Florida, 1704
February 2	Fr. Jean-François Buisson de Saint-Côme, M.E.P.	Louisiana, 1706
February 8	Fr. Didace (Joseph Leon) Arcand, O.F.M.	China, 1951
February 10	Fr. Benjamin Marie Petit	Missouri, 1839
February 14	Fr. Luis Quirós, S.J.	Virginia, 1571
February 14	Br. Gabriel de Sólis, S.J.	Virginia, 1571
February 14	Novice Juan Bautista Mendez, S.J.	Virginia, 1571
February 18	Fr. Juan Bautista de Segura, S.J.	Virginia, 1571
February 18	Novice Cristobal Redondo, S.J.	Virginia, 1571
February 18	Br. Pedro Linares, S.J.	Virginia, 1571
February 18	Br. Gabriel Gómez, S.J.	Virginia, 1571
February 18	Br. Sancho Ceballos, S.J.	Virginia, 1571
February 20	Fr. Leonard Vatier, O.F.M.	Wisconsin, 1715

February 21	Bishop Francis Xavier Ford, M.M.	China, 1952
February 22	Fr. Francisco Letrado, O.F.M.	New Mexico, 1631
February 23	Fr. Leo Heinrichs, O.F.M.	Colorado, 1908
February 27	Fr. Martín de Arvide, O.F.M.	New Mexico, 1631
March 2	An unknown Franciscan	Florida, 1697
March 2	An unknown Indian chief	Florida, 1697
March 3	Fr. Juan Minguez, O.F.M.	Nebraska, 1720
March 10	Frances Gonannhatenha, Indian	New York, 1680
March 16	Fr. Alonso Giraldo de Terreros, O.F.M.	Texas, 1758
March 16	St. Jean de Brébeuf, S.J.	Québec, 1649
March 16	Fr. José Santiesteban, O.F.M.	Texas, 1758
March 16	St. Gabriel Lalemant, S.J.	Ontario, 1649
March 20	Fr. Gaston	Illinois, 1730
March 24	Fr. Chefdeville, S.S.	Texas, 1689
March 24	Fr. Zénobe Membré, O.F.M.	Texas, 1689
March 24	Fr. Maxim Le Clercq, O.F.M.	Texas, 1689
March 25	Fr. Antoine Senat, S.J.[102]	Mississippi, 1736
March 25	Commander Pierre d'Artiquette	Mississippi, 1736
March 25	Capt. Francis Marie Bissot de Vincennes	Mississippi, 1736
March 25	Capt. Louis Dailebout de Coulonge	Mississippi, 1736
March 25	Capt. Louis Charles du Tisne	Mississippi, 1736
March 25	Capt. François Mariauchau d'Esgly	Mississippi, 1736
March 25	Capt. Pierre Antoine de Tonty	Mississippi, 1736
March 25	Capt. Louis Groston de St. Ange, Jr.	Mississippi, 1736
April 17	Fr. Jacques Gravier, S.J.	Louisiana, 1708
April 18	Br. José Pita, O.F.M.	Texas, 1721
April 19	Br. Luis Descalona de Ubeda, O.F.M.	New Mexico, 1542
April 20	Br. Louis Le Boesme, S.J.	Wisconsin, 1687
April 26	Fr. Jacques Gravier, S.J.	Alabama, 1708
c. May 1	Fr. Juan de Padilla, O.F.M.	Kansas, 1542
c. May 4	Fr. Diego de la Cruz, O.P.	Texas, 1554
c. May 6	Fr. Hernando Méndez, O.P.	Texas, 1554
c. May 7	Br. Juan de Mena, O.P.	Texas, 1554

May 10	Fr. Jacques Buteux, S.J. | Québec, 1652
May 10	Pierre Fontarabie, layman | Québec, 1652
May 11	Fr. José Francisco Ganzabal, O.F.M. | Texas, 1752
May 12	Fr. Francisco Lopez, O.F.M. | New Mexico, 1582
May 20	Br. Augustin Rodriguez, O.F.M. | New Mexico, 1582
May 23	Fr. Emil Kapaun | Korea, 1951
May 29	Br. Jean Liégeois, S.J. | Québec, 1655
June 4	Fr. Jose de Arbizu, O.F.M. | New Mexico, 1696
June 4	Fr. Antonio Carbonel, O.F.M. | New Mexico, 1696
June 5	Fr. Francisco de Jesus Maria Casañas, O.F.M. | New Mexico, 1696
June 8	Fr. Francisco Corvera, O.F.M. | New Mexico, 1696
June 8	Fr. Antonio Moreno, O.F.M. | New Mexico, 1696
June 6	Fr. Jean-Pierre Aulneau de la Touche, S.J. | Ontario, 1736
June 12	Fr. Diego de Peñalosa, O.P. |Florida, 1549
c. June 17	Fr. Diego de Tolosa, O.P. | Florida, 1549
c. June 17	Br. Fuentes, O.P. | Florida, 1549
June 21	Fr. Nicholas Benoît Constantin de le Halle, O.F.M. | Michigan, 1706
June 25	Fr. Nicholas Viel, O.F.M., Rec. | Québec, 1625
June 25	Ahuntsic, Indian | Québec, 1625
June 26	Fr. Luis Cáncer de Barbastro, O.P. | Florida, 1549
June 28	Fr. Francisco Porras, O.F.M. | New Mexico, 1631
June 30	Bl. Vasel Velychkovsky, C.SS.R. | Manitoba, 1973
July 4	Fr. Francisco de Bassost, O.F.M. Cap. | California, 1872
July 5	Fr. Francisco X. Silva, O.F.M.[103] | Texas, 1749
c. July 6	Fr. James Maginn, S.S.C. | Korea, 1950
July 14	St. Kateri Tekakwitha | Québec, 1680
July 17	Fr. Juan M. Diaz, O.F.M. | California, 1781
July 17	Fr. José Matias Moreno, O.F.M. | California, 1781
July 17	Fr. Juan A. Barrenche, O.F.M. | California, 1781
July 19	Fr. Francisco H. Garcés, O.F.M. | California, 1781
August 7	Fr. Pedro de Avila y Ayala, O.F.M. | New Mexico, 1672
August 9	Fr. Jean Daniel Têtu | Louisiana, 1718

August 10	Fr. Juan Bautista de Pío, O.F.M. | New Mexico, 1680
August 10	Fr. Juan Bernal, O.F.M. | New Mexico, 1680
August 10	Fr. Domingo de Vera, O.F.M. | New Mexico, 1680
August 10	Fr. Ferdinando de Velasco, O.F.M. | New Mexico, 1680
August 10	Fr. Juan de Jesus, O.F.M. | New Mexico, 1680
August 10	Fr. Tomás de Torres, O.F.M. | New Mexico, 1680
August 10	Fr. Mateo Rendon, O.F.M. | New Mexico, 1680
August 10	Bartolomé Naranjo, Indian | New Mexico, 1680
August 11	Fr. Juan de Jesús, O.F.M. | New Mexico, 1680
August 11	Fr. Lucas Maldonado, O.F.M. | New Mexico, 1680
August 11	Fr. Juan de Val, O.F.M. | New Mexico, 1680
August 11	Fr. Antonio de Mora, O.F.M. | New Mexico, 1680
August 11	Br. Juan de la Pedrosa, O.F.M. | New Mexico, 1680
August 11	Fr. Emanuel Tinoco, O.F.M. | New Mexico, 1680
August 11	Fr. Luis de Morales, O.F.M. | New Mexico, 1680
August 11	Br. Antonio Sanchez de Pro, O.F.M. | New Mexico, 1680
August 11	Br. Luis de Baeza, O.F.M. | New Mexico, 1680
August 11	Fr. Juan del Val, O.F.M. | New Mexico, 1680
August 11	Fr. James Coyle | Alabama, 1921
August 11	Fr. Ángel Baráibar y Moreno | Spain, 1936
August 12	Fr. José de Figueroa, O.F.M. | Arizona, 1680
August 12	Fr. Francisco Antonio de Lorenzana, O.F.M. | New Mexico, 1680
August 12	Fr. Juan de Talaban, O.F.M. | New Mexico, 1680
August 12	Fr. José de Montesdoca, O.F.M. | New Mexico, 1680
August 12	Fr. Lorenzo Analisa, O.F.M. | New Mexico, 1680
August 12	Fr. Juan Espinosa, O.F.M. | New Mexico, 1680
August 12	Br. Sebastian Casalda, O.F.M. | New Mexico, 1680
August 12	Fr. José de Trujillo, O.F.M. | New Mexico, 1680
August 14	Fr. René Menard, S.J. | Wisconsin, 1661
c. August 15	Msgr. Patrick Brennan, S.S.C. | Korea, 1950
August 23	Fr. Sébastien Râle, S.J. | Maine, 1724
August 26	A Jesuit priest and three laymen | Québec, 1644
August 29	Fr. Jacques le Maître, Sulpician | Québec, 1661

August 31   Fr. José de Espeleta, O.F.M. | New Mexico, 1680

August 31   Fr. Augustin de Santa Maria, O.F.M. | New Mexico, 1680

September 2   Fr. Leonard Garreau, S.J. | Quebec, 1656

September 2   Bl. André Grasset | France, 792

c. September   Margaret Garangouas, Indian | New York, 1693

c. September   Infant son of Margaret Garangouas, Indian | New York, 1693

September 10   Fr. Juan de Santa Maria, O.F.M. | New Mexico, 1582

September 11   François Danbourné, layman | Mississippi, 1702

September 11   Two nameless lay Canadians | Mississippi, 1702

September 11   Fr. Nicolas Foucault, M.E.P. | Mississippi, 1702

September 12   Fr. Alphonse L'Heureux, O.C.S.O. | China, 1947

September 13   Fr. Pedro de Corpa, O.F.M. | Georgia, 1597

September 14   Fr. Juan de Silva, O.F.M. | Georgia, 1597

September 15   Fr. Francisco Verascola, O.F.M. | Georgia, 1597

September 16   Fr. Blas de Rodríguez, O.F.M. | Georgia, 1597

September 17   Fr. Miguel de Auñón, O.F.M. | Georgia, 1597

September 17   Br. Antonio de Badajoz, O.F.M. | Georgia, 1597

September 19   Fr. Gabriel de la Ribourde, O.F.M., Rec. | Illinois, 1680

September 29   St. René Goupil, S.J. | New York, 1642

September 28   Bl. Nykyta Budka | Ukraine, 1949

September 29   Fr. Guillaume Vignal, P.S.S. | Québec, 1661

September 29   Two Jesuit Fathers | Wisconsin, 1765

September 30   Br. Gilbert du Thet, S.J. | Maine, 1613

October 6   Fr. Pedro de Martínez, S.J. | Florida, 1566

October 12   Fr. Andrés Quintana, O.F.M. | California, 1812

October 18   St. Isaac Jogues, S.J. | New York, 1646

October 18   St. Jean de Lalande, S.J. | New York, 1646

October 25   Stephen te Gananokoa, Indian | New York, 1680

November 4   Fr. Luis Jayme, O.F.M. | California, 1775

November 4   Fr. José Antonio Díaz de León, O.F.M. | Texas, 1834

November 10   Fr. Jean Dequerre, S.J. | Illinois, 1661

November 16   Ann Glover | Massachusetts, 1688

November 21   Fr. Enrique Ruhen, S.J. | Arizona, 1751

November 25   Fr. Juan de la Cruz, O.F.M. | Texas, 1544
November 25   Bishop Patrick Byrne, M.M. | Korea, 1950
November 28   Fr. Paul du Poisson, S.J. | Mississippi, 1736
December 7   Three unknown Franciscans | Florida, 1647
December 7   St. Charles Garnier, S.J. | Ontario, 1649
December 7   St. Antoine Daniel, S.J. | Québec, 1649
December 8   St. Nöel (Natalis) Chabanel, S.J. | Québec, 1649
December 11   Fr. Jean Souel, S.J. | Mississippi, 1729
December 16   Fr. Sandy Cairns, M.M. | China, 1941
December 28   Fr. Pedro Miranda, O.F.M. | New Mexico, 1631
December 28   Fr. Domingo de Saraoz, O.F.M. | New Mexico, 1639
December 28   Fr. Diego de San Lucas, O.F.M. | New Mexico, 1639

No date: Fr. Christopher Plunkett, O.F.M. Cap. | Virginia, 1697
               Br. Luis de Montesdoca, O.F.M. | Texas, 1718

Did George Washington Die a Catholic?

On a different note, here is another thing you probably didn't know about U.S. history: George Washington may have died a Catholic. We have no smoking gun for this claim, but there is some intriguing circumstantial evidence.

First, though, let's consider the opposing arguments. Washington biographer Joseph Ellis asserts no prayers were said or Christian rites intoned at the president's deathbed, mainly because, he claims, no ministers were present. In fact, the dying Washington's biggest concern was that he not be buried alive. Thus, he stipulated that three days should elapse between his death and his burial.[104]

Others say that Washington wouldn't have cared for deathbed prayer, given what they contend were his quasi-Deist/quasi-Anglican beliefs. That is, they assert he cared little for Christianity, although he strongly believed in God.[105]

Even if this assertion is true—and there is plenty of evidence to doubt that it is—we do know that by the time he died, Washington was no longer anti-Catholic as he was earlier in his life. After all, in 1775 he banned the Continental Army's observance of Guy Fawkes Day, with its ritual burning of the pope in effigy. His two aides-de-camp were Catholic. He was friends with a Spanish spy who died during the war and whose funeral Mass Congress, mostly under Washington's influence, attended almost to a man. Washington counted the Marquis de Lafayette as another friend.[106]

As president, the man Pope Leo XIII (1878–1903) would call "the great Washington" occasionally attended Mass at Philadelphia's St. Mary Church. One report says he contributed to the building of the same city's St. Augustine Church. His many dinner guests noticed him crossing himself before grace, though it should be noted that Anglicans never jettisoned the Sign of the Cross as did other Protestants.

At Washington's death, he possessed pictures of St. John and the Blessed Virgin. Additionally, his Protestant slaves were quite distressed because their master had gone over to the "whore of Babylon."

The Maryland Province Jesuits have historically believed the claim that Washington died a Catholic. The reason? One of their own performed the baptism: Fr. Leonard Neale, chaplain at St. Mary Mission, across the river from Mount Vernon. Furthermore, Washington's first cousin three times removed once claimed it a family tradition that her relative had died a convert.

St. Katharine Drexel's biographer Ellen Tarry says that from childhood Katharine prayed fervently for George Washington's soul.[107] Katharine was born less than sixty years after Washington's passing, and at the time, Catholics were not disposed to pray for the souls of those outside the Church.

Fr. Edward Sorin, C.S.C., founder of the University of Notre Dame, named the school's buildings exclusively after saints and other Catholic figures. So why did he name Washington Hall after the father of his country?

Washington's letters and diaries might have shed light on this issue. However, his secretary Colonel Tobias Lear destroyed several letters. Large numbers of pages are also missing from the president's diaries, a fact that became apparent only when Lear sent the diaries to Supreme Court Chief Justice John Marshall, who wanted to write a biography of the first founder.

Whether the missing pages and letters touched on religion no one can say, obviously. However, given the then-prevailing prejudice against Catholicism, it is possible that Lear destroyed these documents because they showed Washington's move toward Rome.

We will probably never know for sure whether Washington died a Catholic, but this question provides an interesting addendum to any look at Catholic history in America.

NOTES

1. Joseph Brean, "Anti-gay pamphleteer asks for Supreme Court do-over on test of hate-speech laws," March 15, 2013, http://news.nationalpost.com.
2. http://www.lifesitenews.com/news/elderly-woman-arrested-for-spraying-holy-water-outside-abortion-center-vide.
3. "Pope Francis hails the contemporary martyrs," April 21, 2013, www.timesofmalta.com.
4. "Juan de Padilla," www.kshs.org.
5. Gene M. Burnett, *Florida's Past: People and Events That Shaped the State,* (Sarasota, Fla.: Pineapple, 1986), 157.
6. Rev. Michael Kenny, S.J., *Pedro Martínez, S.J.: Martyr of Florida, 1566: Jesuit Protomartyr of the New World* (St. Leo, Fla.: Abbey, 1939), 6.
7. Kenny, 7.
8. Kenny, 7.
9. Kenny, 11.
10. John R. Swanton, *Early History of the Creek Indians and Their Neighbors,* vol. 73, *Smithsonian Institution Bureau of American Ethnology* (Washington, D.C.: Government Printing Office, 1922), 85, http://books.google.com.
11. Paul Thigpen, "The Georgia Martyrs: Heroic Witnesses to the Sanctity of Marriage," http://www.catholicculture.org.
12. Precisely speaking, martyrdom occurs when someone is put to death *in odium fidei*—that is, because of hatred of the faith.
13. George Davis, *Serpent Wind: Inspired by the True Story of a Small Texas War* (Bloomington, Ind.: Authorhouse, 2007), 63.
14. Peter Guilday, *The Life and Times of John Carroll* (Westminster, Md.: Newman, 1954), 76.
15. Guilday, 77.
16. Guilday, 78–79.
17. Guilday, 79.
18. Guilday, 94.
19. Guilday, 104.
20. Daniel Sargent, *Catherine Tekakwitha* (New York: Longmans, Green, 1937), 131.
21. Sargent, 117.
22. Sargent, 118.

23. Sargent, 130.
24. Sargent, 132.
25. Fr. John Laux, M.A., *Church History* (New York: Benziger, 1989), 475.
26. Laux, 169.
27. Daniel L. Lowery, *Day by Day Through Lent* (Liguori, Mo.: Liguori, 1983), 134.
28. See "Pueblo Rebellion," www.desertusa.com.
29. Letter of the governor and captain-general, Don Antonio de Otermin, "The Pueblo Revolt," in *Archives of the West*, http://www.pbs.org.
30. According to historian Harold Dijon, a "woman employed in the Goodwin household [found the missing clothing] 'stuck under a wardrobe.'" See *Ave Maria*, vol. LX, no. 9, March 4, 1905, 268.
31. Cotton Mather, *Memorable Providences, Relating to Witchcrafts and Possessions,* sect. V, http://law2.umkc.edu.
32. Cotton Mather, *Magnalia Christi Americana, or The Ecclesiastical History of New England, From Its First Planting in the Year 1620, Unto the Year of the Lord 1698* (London: Thomas Parihurst, 1702), bk. 7, 71, p. 667 of the PDF at http://archive.org/details/magnaliachristia00math.
33. Harold Dijon, "A Forgotten Heroine," *The Ave Maria*, vol. LX, no. 9 (March 4, 1905), 266–267.
34. George Francis O'Dwyer, "Ann Glover, First Martyr to the Faith in New England," in Thomas F. Meehan, Stephen Farrelly, Joseph F. Delany, eds., *Historical Records and Studies* (New York: United States Catholic Historical Society, 1921), vol. 15, 70–78, http://books.google.com.
35. Mather, *Magnalia Christi Americana*, 667.
36. Fr. Vincent A. Lapomarda, S.J., "A Catholic in Puritan Society," *American Benedictine Review*, vol. 41, no. 2 (June 1990), 195.
37. Lapomarda, 199.
38. Lapomarda, 197.
39. Robert Calef, *More Wonders of the Invisible World* (Salem, Mass.: Cushing and Appleton, 1823), 299.
40. O'Dwyer, 75.
41. Doran Hurley, "God Bless Her," *The Sign*, June 1950, 52.
42. Mather, *Memorable Providences, Relating to Witchcrafts and Possessions*, sect. X.
43. O'Dwyer, 77.
44. Hurley, 52.

45. *The Catholic Historical Review,* vol. 6 (Washington, D.C.: Catholic University of America, 1921), 496.

46. *Catholic Historical Review,* vol. 6, 497.

47. William A. Clark, "The Church at Nanrantsouak: Sébastien Râle, S.J., and the Wabanaki of Maine's Kennebec River," *The Catholic Historical Review,* vol. 92, no. 3 (July 2006), 225–251, www.uvm.edu.

48. Clark, 234.

49. Zephyrin Engelhardt, *San Diego Mission,* (San Francisco: James H. Barry, 1920), 54, http://books.google.com.

50. Francis J. Weber, "The Death of Fray Luís Jayme Two Hundredth Anniversary," in James E. Moss, ed., *The Journal of San Diego History: San Diego Historical Society Quarterly,* vol. 22, no. 1 (Winter 1976), http://www.sandiegohistory.org.

51. Author's interview with Dr. Bill Watson, August 27, 2012.

52. Watson.

53. Watson.

54. Nicolas-Edme Restif de la Bretonne, *Les nuits de Paris* (Paris: Hachette, 1960), 247–253, http://chnm.gmu.edu.

55. http://translate.google.com/translate?sl=fr&tl=en&js=n&prev=_t&hl=en &ie=UTF-8&u=http%3A%2F%2Ffr.wikipedia.org%2Fwiki%2FPrison _des_Carmes.

56. See Michael Williams, *The Shadow of the Pope* (New York: Whittlesey, 1932), 144.

57. "Priest Shot Dead at Communion Rails: Anarchist Glories in Crime..." *The New York Times,* February 24, 1908, p. 1. http://query.nytimes.com.

58. "Priest Shot Dead."

59. Wayne Fling, "Religion in Alabama," February 24, 2012, www.encyclopedia ofalabama.org.

60. "Stephenson is bound over to grand jury after preliminary," *The Miami Daily Metropolis,* August 21, 1921.

61. For example, see Bl. Vicente Vilar David's story in *39 New Saints You Should Know* (Cincinnati: Servant, 2010), 20.

62. http://www.persecucionreligiosa.es/toledo/t_martires.html.The original quote is, "Antes de la guerra 'el simple hecho de ir a la iglesia y cumplir con los deberes religiosos era algo heroico; siendo sacerdotes y católicos constantemente vejados por la juventud envenenada.'"

63. John Joseph Considine, *When the Sorghum Was High* (New York: Longmans, Green, 1940), 28.
64. Considine, 46.
65. Considine, 108.
66. Considine, 123 (emphasis in the original).
67. Considine, 117.
68. See Filomeno Baptista, *"Nossa Gente," Lusitano Bulletin*, p. 14, http://www.lusitanousa.org.
69. "Rev. 'Sandy' Cairns Slain As Prisoner," *The New York Times*, September 5, 1946, 22.
70. Richard Reid and Edward J. Moffett, *Three Days to Eternity* (Westminster, Md.: n.p., 1956), 96.
71. James Myers, *Enemies Without Guns: The Catholic Church in China* (New York: Paragon, 1991), 12.
72. A prefect apostolic is akin to a diocesan bishop for an area that is not yet a see, that is, not yet a diocese.
73. An apostolic visitor is like a temporary ambassador or investigator.
74. Fr. Philip Crosbie, S.S.C., *March Till They Die* (Dublin: Browne & Nolan, 1955), 57.
75. General absolution occurs when a penitent or group thereof receive(s) absolution without actually having to articulate their sins because the priest cannot hear individual confessions for some legitimate reason. It is only valid in certain extraordinary circumstances (for example, the imminent danger of death). However, once one can personally confess, one must.
76. "Bishop Patrick Byrne, M.M.—Modern martyr of Korea," www.youtube.com.
77. Lane, 249.
78. John Chung Jae-sun and Joseph Kim Chang-mun, eds., *Catholic Korea: Yesterday and Today* (Seoul: Catholic Korea, 1964), 377.
79. Author's interview with Bob Wood, May 20, 2013.
80. The PLA and KPA faced not only ROK and U.S. forces but also those from a host of nations, such as Turkey and Belgium, because the United Nations had determined shortly after the war's outbreak that the DPRK was the aggressor nation. The UN thus committed troops under its aegis to defeat the DPRK.
81. Wood.
82. Wood.

83. Roy Wenzl, "Nine of Kapaun's fellow POWs to witness awarding of Medal of Honor," *The Wichita Eagle,* April 10, 2013, www.kansas.com.

84. Wood.

85. Author's interview with Mike Dowe, May 30, 2013.

86. Dowe.

87. Wood.

88. Dowe.

89. Dowe.

90. Wood.

91. Wood.

92. Dowe.

93. Remarks by President Barack Obama at Presentation of the Medal of Honor to Chaplain Emil J. Kapaun, April 11, 2013, www.whitehouse.gov.

94. Eric Veillette, "Père Didace, martyr en Chine," September 9, 2010, http://historiquementlogique.com, author's translation.

95. George Weigel, "Why Hasn't Francis Ford Been Beatified? *First Things,* July 27, 2011, www.firstthings.com.

96. Brian O'Neel, *39 New Saints You Should Know* (Cincinnati: Servant, 2010), 100.

97. O'Neel, 102.

98. Dean Wright, director; *For Greater Glory: The True Story of Christiada;* Arc Entertainment, 2012.

99. http://www.augustinianyouthireland.com/augustinianorder/saintsand blesseds.html.

100. www.reocities.com/Athens/1534/saints/nieves.htm.

101. Fr. Juan de Parga was buried at San Lorenzo Ibitachuco, near Lamont, Madison County, Florida.

102. Fr. Senat was burned at Pontoc, near Fulton, Mississippi.

103. Fr. Silva was buried at San Juan Bautista Mission across from Eagle Pass, Texas.

104. See Joseph Ellis, *His Excellency: George Washington* (New York: Vintage, 2004), 268–270.

105. http://bibowen.hubpages.com/hub/Washington-Deist and http://en.wikipedia.org/wiki/George_Washington_and_religion.

106. http://www.barnesandnoble.com/w/revolutionary-friends-selene-castrovilla/
1113793926?ean=9781590788806 and http://www.mountvernon.org/educa-
tional-resources/encyclopedia/washington-lafayette and http://wiki.answers.
com/Q/Was_marquis_de_lafayette_catholic.

107. See Ellen Tarry, *St. Katharine Drexel: Friend of the Oppressed* (San Francisco:
Ignatius, 2002), 20, 34.

About the Author

Brian O'Neel is a speaker, freelance editor and writer, and Catholic journalist. He has had over two hundred articles published, has helped publish seven books, and is the author of *39 New Saints You Should Know* and *Saint Who? 39 Holy Unknowns*.

Those interested in commenting on *150 North American Martyrs You Should Know*, booking Brian for speaking engagements, radio and television appearances, or book signings, or working with him on their writing and editing projects may contact him at CatholicPbWriter@ yahoo.com.